FROM THE LIBRARY OF

CIRCLING
the
DRAIN
by evan dorkin

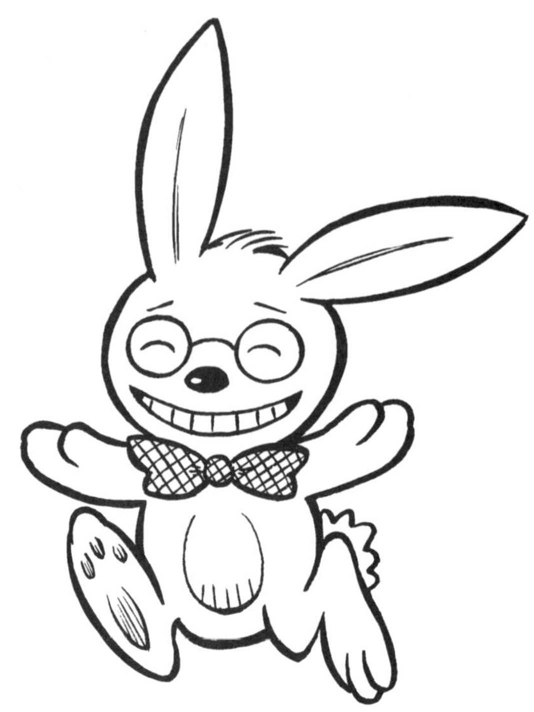

The Collected *Dork*, Volume 2: *Circling the Drain*

For Sarah

Most of the material in this book has been compiled from *Dork* #7-10, published by Slave Labor Graphics, 1999-2002. The following strips appeared in other comics anthologies, magazines and fanzines prior to appearing in *Dork,* and are listed here along with the original source of their publication:

"Advertising Spokescharacters of Yesteryear" – *Instant Piano* #2 (Dark Horse Comics), Dec 1994
"What Does it Look Like I'm Doing?" - *Instant Piano* # 4 (Dark Horse Comics), June 1995
Murder Can Be Fun #1 cover (Slave Labor Graphics), Feb 1996
"Murder Can Be Fun" – *Murder Can Be Fun* # 6 (Slave Labor Graphics), July 1997
"Murder Can Still Be Fun" – *Murder Can Be Fun* # 7 (Slave Labor Graphics), Sept 1997
"Our Days Are Numbered" – *Murder Can Be Fun* # 8 (Slave Labor Graphics), Jan 1998
"Rock, Paper, Scissors" – *Scatterbrain* #3 - (Dark Horse Comics), Aug 1998
"Fisher Price Theatre Presents George Orwell's 1984" – *Scatterbrain* # 4 (Dark Horse Comics), Sept 1998
The Comics Journal #214 cover (Fantagraphics), July 1999
"The Soda Thief" – *Streetwise* (TwoMorrows), July 2000

Editor, co-designer, cover colorist and pre-press assembly – Sarah Dyer
President and Publisher, SLG – Dan Vado
Editor-In-Chief, SLG – Jennifer de Guzman

Published by Slave Labor Graphics – PO Box 26427, San Jose, CA 95159-6427

Printed in Canada

First Printing - June, 2003

ISBN # 0-943151-70-8

Table of Contents

Introduction 6
The Invisible College of Secret Knowledge (session two) 9
Fun! 15
The Soda Thief 24
The Murder Family in "April Funeral's Day" 27
Advertising Spokescharacters of Yesteryear 33
The Island of Misfit Candy 34
More Advertising Spokescharacters of Yesteryear 36
How To Get Your Ass Kicked in 3 E-Z Lessons 38
The Invisible College of Secret Knowledge (session three) 43
Mighty Carl Jung 51
What Does It Look Like I'm Doing? / Cluttered Like My Head 55
A Few Words About That Last Story 79
For the Love of God 81
Fisher Price Theatre Presents: George Orwell's 1984 83
Rock Paper Scissors 85
Cartoonist Goes to Hell 86
New and Used 88
Cover Gallery and Odds & Ends 90

CIRCLIN' THE DRAIN INTRO-- TAKE ONE!
CLACK!
CIRCLING the DRAIN
EVAN DORKIN
TAKE 1
DATE 5-30-03

UM, HI. MY NAME IS EVAN DORKIN, AND I'M HERE TO INTRODUCE YOU TO MY LATEST BOOK, "CIRCLING THE DRAIN."
TSK, TSK, TSK.
HOW SAD.

EXCUSE ME? WHAT'S THAT SUPPOSED TO MEAN?
HAVING TO INTRODUCE YOUR OWN BOOK. RATHER PATHETIC, WOULDN'T YOU SAY?
WELL, NO, I WOULDN'T.
NOT IN PUBLIC, AT LEAST.

ANYWAY, THIS VOLUME COLLECTS ALL OF DORK #7-10, SAVE FOR THE "ELTINGVILLE CLUB" STRIPS, WHICH WILL BE COLLECTED IN A SINGLE, COMPLETE VOLUME IN THE NEAR FUTURE.
THAT'S WHAT YOU SAID IN THE LAST BOOK.
TWO YEARS AGO.

HEH HEH HEH.
BITTER LITTLE PUPPET, IT'S TIME TO SHUT UP.
MMPH! MM-MMPH! *
* BITING SARCASM AIMED AT AUTHOR.

HMM. NOW THAT I THINK OF IT, THERE ISN'T MUCH TO INTRODUCE HERE. IT'S JUST A BUNCH OF GOOFY COMICS. I COULD TALK ABOUT DORK #7, BUT I THINK I'D RATHER DISCUSS THAT LATER ON IN THE BOOK.
=YAWN=

WHY NOT THANK THE PEOPLE WHO HELPED MAKE THIS QUESTIONABLE AFFAIR POSSIBLE?

YOU MEAN, LIKE THE FOLKS WHO COMMISSIONED SOME OF THE WORK, OR OFFERED ME WORDS OF ADVICE OR ENCOURAGEMENT?

YES. YOUR ENABLERS, AS IT WERE.

LET'S SEE, WELL, THERE'S BOB SCHRECK, SCOTT ALLIE, JOHN MORROW, STEPHEN DeSTEFANO, ROBBIE BUSCH, JOHN MARR, DAVID MAZZUCCHELLI, BOB FINGERMAN, BILL KOROSH, TOM SPURGEON & RICH KREINER.

I ESPECIALLY WANT TO THANK CRAIG PAPE AND BOB SIMPKINS, AND OF COURSE, DAN VADO. LAST, BUT NOT LEAST, MY DEEPEST APPRECIATION GOES TO MY WIFE, BEST FRIEND AND PARTNER IN CRIME, SARAH DYER. NOT ONLY FOR HER TREMENDOUS SUPPORT, BUT, WELL, JUST FOR PUTTING UP WITH ME.

YOU'LL SEE WHAT I MEAN WHEN YOU READ THE BOOK ...
HMM, YES, IT TRULY IS A MIRACLE THAT YOU HAVEN'T AWAKENED ONE GRAY AFTERNOON IN CRIMSON SHEETS, A STEAK KNIFE HILT-DEEP IN YOUR CHEST--

AHEM! WELL, I'M GETTING THE SIGNAL THAT WE'RE OUT OF TIME! SO, LET ME WRAP THIS MESS UP BY THANKING YOU FOR BUYING, BORROWING OR STEALING THIS BOOK. I CERTAINLY HOPE YOU GET A LAUGH FROM IT.
*

* UNCHARACTERISTICALLY VILE THREAT AIMED AT AUTHOR

WELCOME BACK, SINNERS
TO THE INVISIBLE COLLEGE
OF SECRET KNOWLEDGE
CLAP HA HA CLAP CLAP CLAP HA HA CLAP
THANK YOU, DEAR FRIENDS. THANK YOU.
YOU ARE ALL ...TOO KIND.
IT PAINS ME TO HAVE TO LEAVE SUCH GOOD COMPANY, BUT THE HOUR IS LATE, AND I MUST BE OFF!

NO, NOT YET! DON'T LEAVE YET!
YEAH, YOU CAN'T LEAVE US YET!
I STILL GOTS HALF A BOTTLE LEFT!
LET'S HAVE ANOTHER STORY!
PLEASE TELL US ANOTHER ONE!
YEAH, PLEASE?
NOW, NOW, SETTLE DOWN GENTLEMEN! I AM NOT A HEARTLESS CREATURE, AND TO PROVE IT I SHALL GRANT YOU ALL A REPRIEVE!
A SHORT REPRIEVE. MIND YOU, FOR IT IS LATE AND MY HOST GROWS WEARY.
B-BLESS YOU, SIR!

NEVERTHELESS, IN THAT SCANT TIME I SHALL GLADLY RELATE TO YOU SEVERAL MORE SHORT TALES OF THOSE UNFORTUNATE SOULS WHO HAVE FOUND THEMSELVES BANISHED BY MAN'S MEMORY AND BLACKLISTED FROM HIS RECORD BOOKS.
THESE ARE HISTORY'S MYSTERY MEN AND WOMEN, POP CULTURE CASTAWAYS FOREVER LOST IN THE FOG OF SOCIETY'S ALZHEIMER'S, THEIR LIVES NEVER TO BE MADE INTO TV MOVIES, THEIR NAMES NEVER TO BE USED AS CLUES TO CROSSWORD PUZZLES, THEIR FACES NEVER TO BE IMMORTALIZED BY THE FRANKLIN MINT.

THEY ARE GHOSTS WHO HAUNT NO ONE, THEIR OWN FAMILY AND FRIENDS DOUBTING THEIR EXISTENCE AS THE HEAVY, EVER-FLOWING YEARS URGE THEM TO SEEK SLEEP RATHER THAN TRUTH.
BUT THEY WALKED THIS EARTH, AND THEY BREATHED HER AIR... AND THOUGH THE WORLD MAY FORGET THEM--
--THE DEVIL PUPPET WILL NOT.

RIGHT, THEN, WHERE DID I LEAVE OFF? I TOLD YOU OF THE UGLY MAN SALOON ... AND MERLE EMERY, THE WOMAN WHO FIRST INSTIGATED THE RATHER CURIOUS PRACTICE OF WASHING CHILDREN'S MOUTHS OUT WITH SOAP...
HAVE I TOLD YOU THE STORY OF "LITTLE METHUSELAH," THE THREE FOOT HIGH "KING OF SUICIDE"?
ER, YES, SIR! LAST CHRISTMAS, WITH THE GYPSIES!

AHH, RIGHT YOU ARE, MAN. MY APOLOGIES.
AH, HERE! I HAVE ONE FOR YOU! IT'S A WHISP, A MERE PUP, BUT WILL DO FOR A START.
NOW, THEN-- WHO HERE HAS HEARD OF THE KISS ARMY?

OH HELL, YEAH! I WAS IN THE KISS ARMY!
ME, TOO! DETROIT ROCK CITY!!
AHH, SCREW THAT! CHEAP TRICK, MAN, ALL THE WAY!

SO THEN, WHO HERE HAS HEARD OF THE KISS NAVY?
KISS NAVY?
WHAT KISS NAVY?!
EXACTLY. BUT YOU CAN REST ASSURED, AS SURE AS I EXIST, THER WAS INDEED SUCH AN ENTITY... THE VERY FEW THE OVERLY PROUD...

THE KISS NAVY.
IN 1978, A TEENAGER NAMED CURTIS HAUGETO OF YONKERS, NEW YORK, FOUNDED THE NAVY AS AN ALTERNATIVE TO THE KISS ARMY. HE SOUGHT TO UNITE FANS OF THE SOFTER SIDE OF THE ROCK BAND, AND THE TREACLY BALLAD "BETH" IN PARTICULAR.
SOME PEOPLE MIGHT GO FOR THE BLOOD AND FIRE-BREATHING..
..BUT I PREFER TO CONCENTRATE ON THE BAND'S ARTISTRY!
BETH I HEAR YOU CALLING
DURING IT'S BRIEF LIFE SPAN, THE GROUP'S RANKS PEAKED AT A PALTRY FOURTEEN MEMBERS NATIONWIDE. APPARENTLY THE AVERAGE KISS FAN WAS SIMPLY NOT ATTRACTED TO THE NAVY'S NARROW FOCUS AND MORE DELICATE AGENDA.
I JUST FEEL PUTTING THEIR BLOOD IN THE INK IS AN UNCALLED FOR GROSS OUT!
AND AS YOUR ADMIRAL, I SAY WE DO NOT SUPPORT THE KISS COMIC BOOK EVEN IF IT IS KISS!
ANYWAY, TODD WILL NOW SHOW US THE CHORD PROGRESSIONS FOR "BETH".
BUT I CAN'T COME HOME RIGHT NOW 'CAUSE ME AND THE BOYS ARE PLAYIN'
CREEM
CRACKED
HAUGETO'S VIGOROUS ATTEMPTS TO RECRUIT NEW MEMBERS INVARIABLY ENDED IN SKIRMISHES WITH HOSTILE MEMBERS OF THE KISS ARMY.
KISS NAVY MY ASS!
I BET YOUR FAVORITE SONG IS "BETH", YOU FAG!
OWW! SO WHAT IF IT IS?! PETER CRISS IS VASTLY- AAARGH!
OH, GOD ...I WISH WE HAD SOME KISS MP'S TO BREAK THIS UP...
KISS 1978 TOUR
KISS ARMY
JOIN THE KISS NAVY
ULTIMATELY, WHAT SANK THE KISS NAVY WAS NOT THE CONSTANT DESERTIONS AND BEATINGS, BUT A CEASE AND DESIST LETTER FROM THE BAND'S LABEL.
B-BUT GUYS.. WE CAN BEAT THIS! WE'RE THE KISS NAVY!
SCREW THAT! I'M SICK OF THIS OUTFIT AN' I'M SICK OF "BETH"! I'M DEFECTIN' TO THE KISS ARMY!
I'M INTO DISCO NOW, ANYWAY!
ME TOO!
WANNA ROLLER-BOOGIE?
MR. HAUGETO NOW WORKS IN A DELAWARE CARPET STORE, AND IN HIS SPARE TIME RUNS A WEBSITE DEVOTED TO THE 80'S CHRISTIAN GLAM-METAL BAND "STRYPER". ALL THAT REMAINS OF THE KISS NAVY IS A DIM MEMORY, AND A SINGLE SURVIVING MEMBERSHIP CARD.
SO, WHERE IS IT?
I'LL MAKE YOU A WAGER, MY FINE GREASEPAINTED FRIEND. YOU SHOW ME WHERE MAN'S FOLLY LIES, AND I'LL SHOW YOU WHERE THE CARD MAY BE FOUND.
Ummm...
uhhhh...
AH, JUST AS I THOUGHT.
HA HA HA HA HA HA HA HA HA HA
NOW, SHALL WE MOVE ON?

IN THE ANNALS OF SCIENCE, THERE HAVE BEEN A NUMBER OF PHYSICISTS, THEORISTS AND OUT AND OUT CRACKPOTS CONSUMED WITH THE NOTION OF CONTROLLING THE MYSTERIOUS PHYSICAL FORCE CALLED GRAVITY.
GRAVITY CONTROL IS NOT ONLY A POSSIBILITY, IT IS A CERTAINTY! MARK MY WORDS!
IN TEN YEARS TIME WE WILL BE ABLE TO SIMPLY TURN GRAVITY ON AND OFF, AS WE DO NOW WITH ELECTRICITY!
ONE SUCH INDIVIDUAL WAS THE NOT SO ESTEEMED DR. EMMANUEL PLITSKY.
1935
WHAT CHEESE!
!
IMBECILIC POPPYCOCK!
FLASH GORDON NONSENSE!
GRAVITY IS A QUALITY OF SPACE!
HA HA
TO CONTROL IT IS IMPOSSIBLE, YOU CRETIN!
AS ONE MIGHT EXPECT, THE SCIENTIFIC COMMUNITY OF THE 1930's CONSIDERED PLITSKY TO BE A LUNATIC.
SUBSCRIBING TO THE THEORIES OF ANTI-GRAVITY "PIONEERS" SUCH AS FRANCIS E. NIPHER AND THOMAS T. BROWN -- WHO POSTULATED THAT ELECTRICAL FIELDS COULD SUSPEND GRAVITY -- PLITSKY SPENT YEARS WRITING PAPERS THAT MET WITH SILENCE
AAAAAA
-AND CONDUCTING EXPERIMENTS THAT MET WITH FAILURE.
IN 1949 PLITSKY FELL IN WITH ROGER BABSON'S NEW HAMPSHIRE BASED GRAVITY RESEARCH FOUNDATION. BABSON, A STOCK MARKET ANALYST AND FORMER PROHIBITION PARTY PRESIDENTIAL CANDIDATE, DESPERATELY SOUGHT SOME KIND OF MATERIAL THAT WOULD NULLIFY GRAVITY THE WAY AN OPAQUE WALL BLOCKED LIGHT.
HELL, EDISON WENT THROUGH EIGHT THOUSAND MATERIALS BEFORE HE HIT ON THE RIGHT ONE FOR A LIGHT BULB FILAMENT!
SO OUR GRAVITY BLOCKER COULD BE ANYTHING! TREATED WOOD, METAL, RUBBER OR CHEMICAL VARNISH OR PAINT OR OIL--
Hmm... PAINT!
UNFORTUNATELY FOR PLITSKY, HIS NEW COLLEAGUES RECEIVED HIS IDEAS EXACTLY AS HIS FORMER PEERS HAD
ANTI-GRAVITY PAINT?! WHAT ROT!
IT'S PERFECTLY SOUND!
USING BROWN'S GRAVITATOR THEORIES TO CONDUCT ELECTRICITY THROUGH MAGNETIZED AND LACQUERED SU-- I WILL ELICIT A GRAVITATIONAL FIELD THAT--
HA HA
HOG-VASH! ZAT IZ CRAZY TALK!
EMBITTERED, PLITSNEY EMBEZZLED FUNDS FROM THE FOUNDATION, AND WITH HIS LONGTIME ASSISTANT, BIAGGIO SANTINI, BEGAN A NEW EXPERIMENT. SEVERAL OBSCURE JOURNALS STATE THAT PLITSKY'S EFFORTS LED TO NAUGHT, AND HE DISAPPEARED IN SHAME AND RUIN.
SEND THE CURRENT THROUGH, SANTINI--
--AND PREPARE! FOR! ANTI-GRAVITY!
HOKAY!
THEY WERE MISTAKEN.
SANTINI! L-LOOK! IT'S WORKING!
WE'RE LIFTING INTO THE AIR! WE'VE DONE IT!
HA HA! IF ONLY THOSE FOOLS COULD SEE ME NOW!
!
HMMMMMMM
UMMM-- OH, I SAY.
I DO BELIEVE WE'VE OVERLOOKED AN IMPORTANT MATTER HERE...
OH GOOD CHRIST, SAVE US!
AAAAA!

AND THERE YOU HAVE IT...SUCCESS
ND THEN DEATH. BUT COULD WE ASK
NY MORE THAN TO DIE FOR TRUTH?
NO... DON'T ANSWER. WE HAVEN'T THE TIME FOR ANYTHING BUT OUR FINAL STORY--A BIT OF BASEBALL TRIVIA YOU WON'T FIND IN THE HALLS OF COOPERSTOWN.

THE TIME IS 1988. THE PLACE, FEVER CREEK, ILLINOIS. OUR PROTAGONIST--ONE FRANKIE SPECK, A ONCE PROMINENT BASEBALL SCOUT WHO HAD FALLEN FROM MAJOR LEAGUE GRACE TO FIND HIMSELF IN THE DEEPEST THICKETS OF THE BUSH LEAGUES.
HOLY CRAP! THE GUY PISSED HISSELF!
I'M S-SORRY! I'M JUST S-SO NERVOUS!
JESUS, FRANKIE! THAT'S THE NINTH SCRUB SONUVABITCH IN A ROW YOU'VE LEFT ON MY DOORSTEP! WHAT GIVES?!
I-I'M SORRY, JERRY! I'LL GET YA A WINNER, PROMISE!
SPECK LONGED TO RETURN TO THE BIG LEAGUES, BUT HIS MEAL TICKET, HIS BIG SCORE, HIS HOT PROSPECT, NEVER MATERIALIZED.

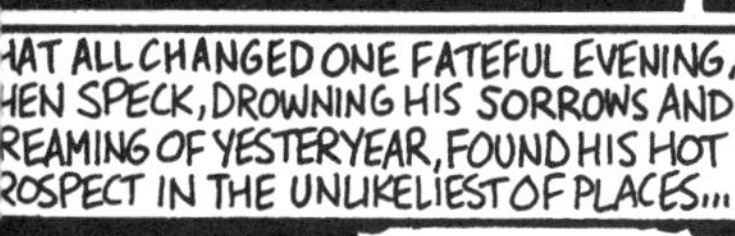

HAT ALL CHANGED ONE FATEFUL EVENING,
HEN SPECK, DROWNING HIS SORROWS AND
REAMING OF YESTERYEAR, FOUND HIS HOT
ROSPECT IN THE UNLIKELIEST OF PLACES...

CNN ISRAEL
VIOLENT PROTESTS CONTINUED TODAY IN ISRAEL AND OCCUPIED PALESTINE AS ANGRY MOBS HURLED ROCKS AND BOTTLES AT ISRAELI SOLDIERS--
BUD
LOOKIT 'EM!
'DON'T SEE THOSE
JYS PISSIN' THEIR
ANTS! THEY STAND
AND DELIVER!

AS THE NEWS FOOTAGE CONTINUED, SPECK BECAME FIXATED ON ONE YOUNG MAN CAUGHT ON CAMERA AMONGST THE CROWD OF ROCK THROWING YOUTHS.
INTIFADA
BUT SOUR
JESUS! WOULD YA LOOK AT THE ARM ON THAT BASTARD? S'LIKE A GODDAM CANNON!
I AIN'T SEEN NO ONE THROW THAT HARD SINCE --SINCE--

SON OF A BITCH!! HAVE I GOT ME AN IDEA! IT'S CRAZY AS SHIT, BUT GOD DAMN IT COULD WORK!

RANDISHING A VIDEOTAPE OBTAINED
ROM AN ACQUAINTANCE AT CNN
PORTS, SPECK FERVENTLY PITCHED
S "CRAZY IDEA" TO HIS EMPLOYEES.
KAY, JERRY,
W WATCH--
HE SAME
ID AGAIN--
POW! PEGGED THAT G.I. JEW AT A HUNDRED FEET, JUST LIKE THE OTHER THREE!
THE KID'S A GODDAM NATURAL, JERRY!
AND NOBODY ON EARTH KNOWS ABOUT HIM! SO--WHADDAYA THINK?!

AS ONE MIGHT EXPECT, SPECK'S IDEA TO SCOUT AN UNKNOWN PALESTINIAN STONE THROWER WAS REJECTED--AS WAS SPECK, WHO WAS DULY FIRED.
UNDAUNTED, SPECK SOLD HIS BASEBALL MEMORABILIA COLLECTION, CALLED IN THE LAST OF HIS FAVORS, AND SET OFF FOR THE MIDDLE EAST--DETERMINED TO FIND HIS "GREAT BROWN HOPE"...
CNN PRESS PASS
...AS WELL AS HIS OWN REDEMPTION.

AFTER HIS ARRIVAL, SPECK SPENT WEEKS SEARCHING FOR THE YOUNG UNKNOWN WITH THE GOLDEN ARM, HIS QUEST TAKING HIM FROM TOWN TO VILLAGE TO REFUGEE CAMP. HIS DREAM AND HIS HIP FLASK HELPED HIM BRAVE RIOTS, ROUND UPS AND GUNFIRE--
--UNTIL THE DAY HIS SEARCH FINALLY PAID OFF.
Ahhh, YES, WE KNOW BASHAR. VERY SAD, HE HAS NO FAMILY.
YEARS AGO THE SOLDIERS BEAT HIM. SINCE THEN, HIS HEAD, YOU KNOW? HE'S A LITTLE CRAZY!
HIS ENGLISH IS VERY BAD. YOU PAY US, WE SPEAK TO HIM FOR YOU!
YOU GOT A DEAL!

SPECK WAS TAKEN TO RAMALLAH, WHERE HE AT LONG LAST MET HIS PROSPECT--A LANKY, ADDLED YOUTH NAMED BASHAR MAAYAH. HE KNEW NOTHING ABOUT BASEBALL, BUT FOR A FEW SHEKELS, HE WAS WILLING TO LEARN.

SON OF A BITCH! ALMOST BROKE MY FRIGGIN' HAND!
BUT THE KID'S GOT IT, ALRIGHT! ALL HE NEEDS IS SOME TRAININ'!
BASE-BALL. HUH.

HOWEVER, SPECK FOUND IT TOOK MORE THAN A FEW COINS TO CONVINCE BASHAR TO TRAVEL TO AMERICA.

--TELL HIM WE GOT MORE THAN BASEBALL! WE GOT SPORTS CARS, CONDOS, WE GOT VIDEO GAMES, McDONALDS, PLAYBOY MAGAZINE, MTV, MADONNA, HBO--
I TELL HIM, BUT HE SAYS NO, HIS HOMELAND NEEDS HIM TO THROW THE JEWS INTO THE SEA--
YEAH, WELL TELL HIM IN AMERICA HE CAN GET A JOB THROWIN' ROCKS THAT'LL MAKE HIM TONS OF MONEY--MONEY HE CAN SEND BACK HOME TO BUY BOMBS AN' GUNS FOR HIS PEOPLE TO KILL ALL THE HEEBS HE WANTS!!
MADONNA ...

SPECK'S NEXT TASK WAS T
EXTRICATE BASHAR FROM T
MIDDLE EAST, A TRICKY
ENDEAVOR WHICH REQUIRE
THE PRESENTATION OF
VARIOUS FALSE DOCUMEN
AS WELL AS THE GREASING
OF VARIOUS PALMS.
$
MVP
$

BACK HOME, SPECK'S LAST HURDLE WAS TO CONVINCE HIS FORMER EMPLOYERS TO GRANT HIS PALESTINIAN SPITFIRE A TRY-OUT.

OKAY, SO HE CAN THROW THE APPLE HARD IN THE POCKET. HOW'S HE AGAINST A BATTER?
WELL, UHH...GEE, ACTUALLY I DUNNO! heh heh!
SON OF A BITCH! MY HAND!
WELL, LET'S FIND OUT! TED--GO TAKE A FEW SWINGS!
HOKAY, COACH!

WHEN MADONNA?
FORGET THAT, OKAY? NOW, LISTEN--SEE THAT GUY OVER THERE? YOU WANNA GET THAT GUY "OUT," SEE? WHEN YOU THROW THE "ROCK," Y'KNOW, THE BALL--HE'S GONNA TRY AN' HIT IT WITH THAT STICK. BUT YOU DON'T WANNA LET HIM HIT IT, BECAUSE HE'S YER ENEMY!
ENEMY?
YEAH, Y'KNOW, LIKE THE JEWS--THE ENEMY, GOT IT?!
ENEMY!!!

BASHAR'S FIRST PITCH STRUC
TED KELLY'S HEAD SO FORCEFUL
THAT HIS HELMET CRACKED IN T
HA!
KELLY'S SKULL WAS CRACKED A
WELL, AND BY THE TIME HE RE
GAINED CONSCIOUSNESS, SPEC
AND BASHAR WERE LONG OUT OF TO

THE PAIR MADE THEIR WAY THROUGH THE BACKWATERS OF THE MID-WEST MINOR LEAGUE CIRCUIT, WHERE BASHAR CONTINUED TO RACK UP PIN STRIPED CASUALTIES.
CRAK
JESUS, NOT AGAIN!
HA! DIE!
DESPITE SPECK'S TRAINING, THE YOUNG MAN'S ARM COULD NOT BE TAMED. HE SIMPLY BEANED EVERYONE HE FACED, UNABLE TO SEPARATE INNOCENT OPPONENTS FROM HATED ENEMIES.

UNABLE TO GIVE UP HIS DREAM, SPECK CONTINUED TO TRAIN HIS PROTEGE. BUT AFTER SUFFERING ENDLESS HEAD INJURIES, FRANKIE SPECK RETIRED FROM BASEBALL AND THIS MORTAL COIL ONE CHILLY SEPTEMBER MORNING.
WHEN MADONNA?
AS FOR BASHAR MAAYAH...WELL, THAT'S ANOTHER STORY IN AND OF ITSELF.

BUT IT WILL HAVE TO WAIT, FOR I MUST TAKE MY LEAVE. NO, DON'T BE SAD.
JUST REMEMB
THIS! YOU HAVE
SPENT TIME WITH
THE DEVIL PUPPE
AND YOU ARE TH
BETTER FOR IT
SO GOOD NIGHT, FELLOW TRAVELLERS. WE WILL MEET AGAIN.

DAS FUNDERKIND!

ev. 98

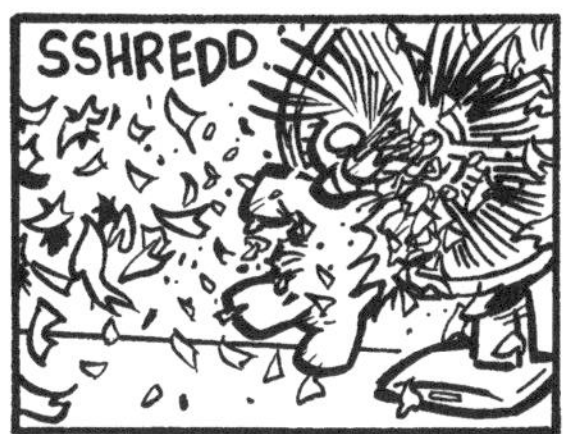

PANIC IN THE YEAR FUN

SCIENCE FICTION THEATRE
presents
THE INCREDIBLE SHIRKING MAN

SO WHA

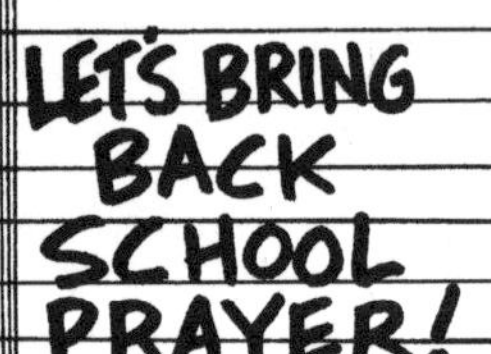

D

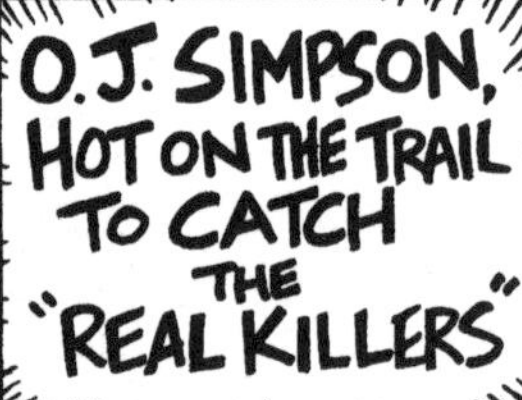

O.J. SIMPSON, HOT ON THE TRAIL TO CATCH THE "REAL KILLERS"

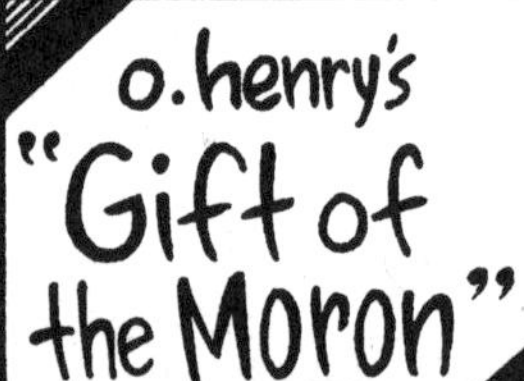

OH, HENRY!

DR. SIDNEY GLICK PHD
WORLD'S WORST PSYCHOTHERAPIST
evan dorkin

BURNE

SHORT STORY WITH A THIN PLOT

THE END

INCOMING FUN!
ev 99

SEIJI NAKIMUSHI, WORLD'S WORST KAMIKAZE PILOT

N-NAKIMUSHI! WHAT ARE YOU DOING HERE?!?

UM... I MISSED.
MISSED?! WHAT DO YOU MEAN YOU MISSED?!

I'LL TRY AGAIN. HONEST I WILL!
I, UM.. I'VE LOST FACE, HAVEN'T I?
BAKA!

MYRON
THE LIVING VOODOO DOLL
© 99 ev

CHUG CHUG

CRUNCH

EEARRGH! THAT @#*?!! DOLL!!

BAD COP / BAD COP

LISTEN OFFICERS, I TOLD YOU I DON'T KNOW ANYTHING!
LOOK YOU-- TELL US WHAT WE WANNA KNOW OR I'LL BREAK YER FUCK'N ARM!

HOLD ON, HOLD ON... LOOK, BUDDY- MY FRIEND HERE HAS A BIT OF A TEMPER. SO WHY DON'T YOU JUST TELL US WHAT WE WANT TO KNOW--

OR I'LL BREAK YER FUCKIN' NECK AN' RAPE Y' WIT' MY NIGHTSTICK!
NO! LET ME CASTRATE HIM!
WAIT YER TURN!

QUASIMODO
PRIVATE INVESTIGATOR
TEL-555-HUGO

"LEFTY" PARKER IS YOUR MAN, LIEUTENANT!

HMMM... "LEFTY" PARKER... YES, THAT RINGS A BELL!
BUT HOW CAN YOU BE SO SURE?

I DON'T KNOW.. IT'S JUST THIS HUNCH THAT I HAVE..
OH CHRIST.
SORRY.

ALFRED IS STILL REALLY DUMB

MY ASS?!
NO YOU MORON!

AT HOME WITH--
ROBERT DOWNEY JR. IN JAIL!

I GOTS TO TELL YA MAN, I LOVED YO' ASS IN "CHAPLIN"!
NOW SERVICING NUMBER 5
OW! OWW! SHIT!

CAN I GETS YO' AUTOGRAPH?
UNNGH!!
HEY-- LOOK EVERYBODY!
OW! GOD!

OH WELL, IT'S STILL BETTER THAN MY YEAR ON SATURDAY NIGHT LIVE!
IT'S THE GUY FROM STONE TEMPLE PILOTS!
OOH.. I GOT DIBS!!
LESS THAN ZERO!

THE MARK OF SORROW

HE CAME FROM OUT OF THE HILLS, LEAVING HIS MARK EVERYWHERE.
LOOK! EETS THE MARK OF SORROW!

SOON, WORD OF HIS DEEDS SPREAD LIKE WILDFIRE THROUGH THE VILLAGE.
HE TOLD ME LIFE IS MEANINGLESS.
HE TOLD ME LOVE IS AN ILLUSION.
HOW DO YOU TELL A FIVE-YEAR OLD THERE IS NO GOD?!

WHO WAS THIS MASKED MAN? WHAT WAS HIS MISSION?!
ALL I KNOW IS HE DEPRESSES ME GREATLY!
SI! I HOPE THE ARMY KEELS HEEM!
AND MUY PRONTO!

SO-CALLED "FUN!"

evan99

SCIENCE FICTION THEATRE presents-
THE VETERINARY PRACTICE OF DR. MOREAU

YOU FIEND! I BROUGHT MY DOG IN FOR A FLEA BATH AND YOU'VE TURNED HIM INTO THIS--THING!

NOT A THING, MADAM! A HUMANIMAL! ISN'T HE MAGNIFICENT? NOT ONLY IS HE FREE OF PARASITES--BUT HE'S A FUNCTIONING, THINKING INDIVIDUAL!
SNIF SNIF
JUST DON'T RILE HIM TOO MUCH.

YOU MANIAC! GIVE ME BACK MY FLUFFY OR I'LL--
PHILISTINE! YOU'LL RUE THIS DAY!

JEW EX-MACHINA

THINGS LOOKED BAD FOR OUR HERO!

BUT THEN, SUDDENLY--

MOSES SAVED HIM!

WHO SAYS I CAN'T WRITE GAGS SHITTY ENOUGH FOR A REAL NEWSPAPER STRIP?

DID I EVER TELL YOU ABOUT MY FRIEND WHO HAD AN ORIGAMI SHOP?

NO, WHAT HAPPENED?

IT FOLDED.
STUKAS

PHIL the DISCO SKINHEAD
HE'S THE BOY WITH CONFLICT!

DAMN! THIS HATE RALLY IS BORING! WHERE THE HELL'S PHIL WITH OUR BEER?
HEY-- HERE HE IS!

HEY, FELLOW PATRIOTS--
WHAT THE FUCK? ST. IDES?! WHERE'S THE COORS, PHIL?!
UHH-- THE BODEGA WAS OUT--
BODEGA?! HEY-- WHAT'S THIS?

VIBE MAGAZINE?! FUCK! KILL THAT RACE TRAITOR!
VIBE

DAD'S A PISSER

HEY, SON--PULL MY FINGER!
OH NO!
NOT THAT ONE AGAIN!

C'MON! PULL MY FINGER!
MOM!
HONEY, PLEASE! NOT AT THE TABLE!!

HA HA HA HA HA!
SGLUSH

SEIJI NAKIMUSHI, WORLD'S WORST KAMIKAZE PILOT

YOU HAVE BROUGHT GREAT SHAME UPON YOURSELF AND YOUR FAMILY! I ORDER YOU TO COMMIT SEPPUKU!
HAI!

OOH! AGH!!

I TRIED-- HONESTLY! BUT THE KNIFE ...SLIPPED.

VOX POPULI
"SO, WHY DID YOU RIOT AT WOODSTOCK 99?"

Y'SEE, SUGAR RAY CANCELLED AND LIKE, MY WORLD COLLAPSED!
SO, LIKE, NOW I GOTTA THROW SHIT!
LIMP

THE, UH, PRICES ARE TOO HIGH! YEAH, THAT'S RIGHT! OH, PLUS I'M DRUNK, STONED AN' FUCKIN' DUMB!
ATM
KORN

KID

THE FUN YOU NEED!

ev00.

BACK IN 1992 I STARTED DOING SOME STRIPS ABOUT CURIOUS GEORGE'S ANGRY AND JEALOUS BROTHER, "FURIOUS GEORGE".

MY BRUDDER CAN SUCK MY WING-WANG. THE FUCK IN THE YELLA HAT, TOO.

SINCE THEN, FURIOUS GEORGE HAS BEEN THE NAME OF A PUNK BAND, A CANADIAN "ULTIMATE" TEAM, AND A GAG ON THE SIMPSONS, AMONG OTHERS.

SO, SAY GOOD-BYE TO FURIOUS GEORGE -- AND HELLO TO: SPURIOUS GEORGE - GREEK ICONOCLAST SHIPPING MAGNATE!

IT WASN'T FUNNY ANYWAY

"PURPLE HAZE"
THE ULTIMATE HENDRIX TRIBUTE

"THAT SMELL"
THE LYNYRD SKYNYRD EXPERIENCE

ROCK OUT!

OH, THE DICHOTOMY!

EERIE!

SO, HOWARD, WHAT DID YOU THINK ABOUT THAT BOOK I LENT YOU?

WITTY!

MON DIEU! EVAIRY TIME I TRY TO MAKE ZEE LOVE, ZEE MADAMES, ZEY TURN TO ZEE STONE AT MY CARESS!

FOR GILBERT H —

¡es muy Funtastico!

evan 00/01

MURDER CAN BE FUN!

VOL. ONE: **ZOO MAYHEM!** INCIDENTS ADAPTED BY evan dorkin FROM JOHN MARR'S **MCBF #16**

5·97

ALASKA ZOO, 1994. KATHRYN WARBURTON DECIDES SHE HAS TO HAVE A CLOSER LOOK AT THE POLAR BEARS--

THE 29 YR. OLD AUSTRALIAN TOURIST AND PART-TIME IMBECILE CLIMBED TWO 3½ FT. FENCES to GET A BETTER LOOK AT 1000 LB. "BINKY."

BINKY ALSO GOT A FEEL FOR KATHRYN.

KATHRYN ESCAPED BINKY'S ATTACK W/A BROKEN LEG AND GASHES. SHE LATER TOLD REPORTERS--

NO DUH!

CLEVELAND ZOO, 1943. A 62-YR. OLD KEEPER IS FOUND DEAD OF A SEVERED JUGULAR IN THE LEOPARD CAGE.

THE ZOO DIRECTOR, WITH A **STRAIGHT FACE**, COULD ONLY SAY:

HINT HINT LEOPARD! CLUE !

THE READER IS FREE TO DRAW HIS OR HER OWN CONCLUSION.

KIDS SURE DO LIKE TO GET REAL CLOSE TO THEM CAGES!

A 6 YR. OLD GIRL TRIES TO PET THE "DOGGIES". THE WOLF PACK MANGLES THE POOR TOT'S ARM AND LATER IT IS AMPUTATED.

1965 - IDAHO FALLS, TAUPHAS PK ZOO

RUTH FREEDMAN, 3, OFFERS WINKIE THE ELEPHANT, 23, SOME POPCORN. PERHAPS OFFENDED BY THE ABSENCE OF BUTTER--

WINKIE WHIPS RUTH to the GROUND WITH HER TRUNK, THEN STOMPS HER.

1966 - MADISON WI, VILAS PK ZOO

JULIA ANN JACKSON, 2½, TEMPTS PASHA the LION (10), WITH PEANUTS. PASHA OPTS FOR JULIA ANN.

1958 - WASH. D.C. NAT'L ZOO

ELEPHANT ASSISTED SUICIDE!

JUMBO KEVORKIAN

THE PACHYDERM IS IN

DURING WWII, A WOMAN WITH A FEW SCREWS LOOSE SNUCK INTO THE PEN OF AN ASIAN BULL ELEPHANT IN THE ZURICH ZOO.

SUICIDE SEEMED TO BE HER GOAL.

THE ASIAN BULL OBLIGED, BY DISMEMBERING AND TRAMPLING HER.

ACCORDING TO REPORTS, THIS LEFT THE BULL WITH A TASTE FOR BLOOD. HE SUPPOSEDLY ATTACKED KEEPERS YRS. LATER, KILLING ONE.

DRIVE-THRU SCALPING!

SLOW 0 M.P.H.

IRVINE'S **LION COUNTRY SAFARI PARK**, 1974

AN ELDERLY WOMAN, EXCITED BY AN APPROACHING **LION**, ROLLS HER CAR WINDOW **DOWN** INSTEAD OF **UP**.

"**TINY**" SCALPED THE HAPLESS OLDSTER BEFORE HE COULD BE FORCED TO LEAVE...

I SAY SEND MORE OLD FOGIES TO THEIR LOCAL SAFARI PARKS!

OR, WHEN HARRY MET SALLY. (AND DIED)

WHEN HAROLD CANNON WENT BACK TO WORK AT ROCHESTER N.Y.'s SENECA PARK ZOO IN 1959, HE DECIDED TO **RENEW** HIS ACQUAINTANCE WITH "**SALLY**".

THOUGH HE'D BEEN GONE A YEAR AND KNEW **SALLY** WAS SKITTISH ABOUT WHO HANDLED HER--

HE ASSUMED SHE'D REMEMBER HIM.

SALLY **DIDN'T** REMEMBER GOOD OLD HAROLD. SHE **TRAMPLED** THE STRANGE INTRUDER TO **DEATH**.

THROWN to THE LIONS!
-OR-
MARTYR CAN BE FUNNY!

WASH. DC's NATIONAL ZOO, 3/95. MARGARET KING, A PARANOID SCHIZO WHO HAD BELIEVED SHE WAS JESUS, IS FOUND MAULED TO DEATH IN THE LION GROTTO.

SHE HAD TO PASS 3 WARNING SIGNS, CLIMB A SMALL FENCE, DROP 9 FEET TO A MOAT, AND SWIM 26 FEET TO FIND DEATH IN THE LION GROTTO.

NO SUICIDE NOTE WAS FOUND, BUT AN AMY GRANT TAPE WAS IN HER WALKMAN. SUICIDE? RELIGIOUS MARTYRDOM? JUST PLAIN **NUTSO**?

MURDER CAN STILL BE FUN!

VOL. TWO: NAUGHTY LITTLE BASTARDS! ADAPTED FROM JOHN MARR'S MURDER CAN BE FUN #17, by evan dorkin 8/97

BABY-SITTING the NAUGHTY WAY!

RICHMOND, 1932. TWO CHILDREN, AGES 6 and 3, WERE BABYSITTING THEIR 10 MONTH OLD SIBLING WHILE THEIR PARENTS WERE AT WORK.

UNFORTUNATELY, CHILDREN THAT AGE AREN'T KNOWN FOR THEIR PATIENCE, AND the BABY CRIED ONCE TOO OFTEN FOR THEIR KIDDIE TASTES.

OF COURSE THE SOLUTION WAS TO SHOVE THE TODDLER INTO A HANDY WOOD STOVE. AH, PEACE AND QUIET

SHUT UP MAW!

HOLSTEIN, IOWA 1930. 14 YR. OLD LESTER MOHR HAD SPENT THE DAY GETTING BLITZED ON ILLICIT BEER.

HIS MOTHER SPOILED HIS BUZZ BY GETTING ON HIS CASE ABOUT SOME HOUSE CHORES HE HADN'T DONE.

OVERREACTING A TAD, LESTER BEAT HER WITH BRICKS, THEN SHOT HER WITH A RIFLE... AND A SHOTGUN.

50 YRS IN PRISON, Y'DUMB HICK.

WHITE PLAINS, NY 1933. 8 YR OLD JOSEPHINE WARDPAY LOVED TO GOSSIP ABOUT the SEXUAL EXPLOITS OF 12-YR OLD MARY KAVALA, A NEIGHBOR.

MARY DID NOT LIKE THIS, ESPECIALLY AS MANY of THESE STORIES WERE TRUE. SO ONE DAY SHE BEAT JOSEPHINE'S GABBY LITTLE CRANIUM TO A PULP.

SHE THEN STRANGLED JOSEPHINE WITH SOME MOP STRANDS.

WHEN MARY CONFESSED, A 46 YR OLD LOVER OF HERS WAS ARRESTED ON A MORALS RAP. JO WAS A GOSSIP, NOT A LIAR

MEADVILLE, PA 1943. GEORGE F. AND HIS PAL CONRAD WERE PLAYING A PLEASANT GAME OF MONOPOLY -- WHEN HOSTILITIES BROKE OUT!

HISTORY DOESN'T RECORD the CAUSE OF THE FRACAS - TAXES? BOARDWALK? WHATEVER... CONRAD HIT GEORGE.

GEORGE RAN HOME, GOT HIS DAD'S REVOLVER AND SHOT CONRAD IN THE HEART, KILLING THE PRETEND TYCOON

KIDS SAY THE STUPIDEST THINGS

THE WIT & WISDOM OF NAUGHTY CHILDREN

NOT SEEN ON THE ART LINKLETTER PROGRAM

I AM TIRED, SICK OF SCHOOL, AND BORED WITH LIFE.

YAWN!

14 YR. OLD EXPLAINING WHY HE ROBBED A STORE AT KNIFEPOINT, 1960

I'D LIKE TO BE A NURSE BECAUSE THEN I CAN STICK NEEDLES IN PEOPLE. I LIKE HURTING PEOPLE.

MARY BELL, 11, MURDERER OF TWO SMALL BOYS AGES 3 AND 4, ENGLAND, 1960

I TOOK the PRAM FROM OUTSIDE the SHOP. THERE WAS A BABY IN the PRAM and I THREW IT IN the WATER. I JUST WANTED to DO IT.

ENGLISH LAD, 9, 1947

IF I KILLED ONE THEY WOULD JUST SEND ME TO REFORM SCHOOLS AGAIN. BUT IF I KILLED THEM BOTH THEY'LL SEND ME TO THE CHAIR.

WANTE

14 YR. OLD EXPLAINING WHY HE HAD TO KILL 2 PLAYMATES, ARKANSAS, 1960

THAT'S WHERE I SHOVED HIM IN.

JAMES B. ON DROWNING A 7 YR. OLD BOY FOR "BEING A SISSY," PHILADELPHIA, PA 1937

I WAS TIRED of WALKING... I THOUGHT I WOULD STOP the TRAIN AND RIDE A WHILE.

16 YR. OLD HARRY SCHERER, ON WHY HE PUT A RAILROAD TIE ACROSS TRACKS, TULSA OK, 1943

HATTIE, AGE 9, HITTING 2 YR. OLD W/AN AXE FOR BITING HER, ≈189

BECAUSE SHE WOULD NOT LET ME GO to the PICTURE SHOW.

BOY'S REASON FOR SHOOTING HIS STEPMOM TO DEATH, FT MYERS FL, 1940

NOTE LEFT by 14 YR OLD BOY WHO SHOT HIS FATHER, 1957

WELSH BOY, 9, AFTER DROWNING A 4-YR. OLD BOY, 1947

MARY BELL, 1960

OUR DAYS ARE NUMBERED!

DISASTER, CALAMITY AND HOMICIDE A LA THE MCBF DATEBOOKS

AN 1 - A SUSPICIOUS FIRE AT A NEW EAR'S EVE SOCIAL CLUB PARTY KILLS 4 PEOPLE, CHAPAIS, QUEBEC, 1979

JAN 3 - A NEWLY CONSTRUCTED CHURCH COLLAPSES DURING MORNING MASS. 58 DEAD, RIJO, MEXICO 1965.

¡madre de dios!

JAN 4 - POT SMOKING CONRAIL ENGINEER RICKY GATES RUNS HIS TRAIN INTO ANOTHER OUTSIDE ESSEX, MD, KILLING 16, 1987

OH MAN! BUMMER!
COACH

JAN 5 - RAIN AND HAIL CAUSE THE PRADO DAM IN ARGENTINA TO FAIL. 27 DIE IN THE ENSUING FLOOD, 1970.

AN 6 - LAWYER JULIAN FRANK IN- URES HIS LIFE FOR $887,500, THEN LOWS UP THE PLANE HE AND 83 OTH- RS ARE ON SO HIS WIFE CAN RE- EIVE THE $. BOLIVIA, N.C, 1960

I DID IT FOR YOU, HONEY!

JAN 7 - A FIRE STARTED BY AN INMATE AT THE MERCY MENTAL HOSP. KILLS 39 FEMALE PATIENTS AND ONE NURSE, DAVENPORT IA, 1950

WHAT ARE YOU, CRAZY?

JAN 8 - AN EXPRESS TRAIN HITS A COMMUTER NEAR WOERDON, HOLLAND, KILLING 92 PASSENGERS, 1962

JAN 9 - BLAMED FOR CAUSING THE PLAGUE, ALL SEVERAL HUNDRED JEWS OF BASEL, SWITZERLAND ARE BURNED TO DEATH IN A SPECIALLY DESIGNED WOODEN HOUSE ON AN ISLAND, 1349

OY VEY!
AGAIN WITH THE BLAME?

AN 10 - DEADLIEST SINGLE AVALANCHE N ESTIMATED 4000 PERUVIANS ARE LLED BY 3 MILLION TONS OF SNOW ROM HUASCARAN MOUNTAIN, 1962

JAN 11 - DAREDEVIL SAMUEL SCOTT ACCIDENTALLY HANGS HIMSELF BEFORE AN EXHIBITION DIVE OFF WATERLOO BRIDGE, LONDON 1841

JAN 12 - HENRY LEE LUCAS COMMITS HIS 1st MURDER, KILLING MOM AFTER AN ARGUMENT OVER VISITING RELATIVES, TECUMSAH MI 1960

JAN 13 - 1st NHL FATALITY. MINNESOTA NORTH STAR ROOKIE BILL MASTERSON SUFFERS A FATAL HEAD INJURY AFTER HE'S CHECKED TO THE ICE, MN, 1968

AN 14 - AN OVERHEATED FUEL TANK THE HOTEL DAE-A SAUNA EXPLODES 8 DIE IN THE BLAST/FIRE, S. KOREA 1984

JAN 16 - CZECH STUDENT JAN PALACH IMMOLATES HIMSELF TO PRO- TEST SOVIET OCCUPATION, HE DIES THREE DAYS LATER, PRAGUE 1969

MAYBE THIS WAS A BAD IDEA...
BURN YOU HIPPY!
GAS

JAN 17 - FRENCH LINER CHAOUIA HITS A LEFTOVER WWI MINE IN THE STRAITS OF MESSINA, 460 PASSENGERS DIE, 1919

JAN 18 - 4 USAF THUNDERBIRD STUNT TEAM JETS FAIL TO PULL OUT OF A LOOP AND CRASH, INDIAN SPRINGS, NV, 1982

AN 19 - A WATER HEATER EXPLOSION LLS 5 CHILDREN AND 1 TEACHER IN A HOOL CAFETERIA, SPENCER OK, 1982

THERE GOES LUNCH!
BOOM

JAN 20 - 303 DROWN WHEN THE KAPUNDA, A BRITISH SHIP, COLLIDES WITH THE ADA MELMORE & SINKS OFF THE BRAZILIAN COAST, 1887

WEREN'T YOU LOOKING?

JAN 21 - AN IRANIAN 727 JET CARRY- ING MOSLEM PILGRIMS CRASHES OUT- SIDE TEHRAN, KILLING 128, 1980

WELL HELLO, ALLAH!

JAN 22 - A 707 CARRYING NIGERIAN MOSLEMS FROM A MECCAN PILGRAMAGE CRASHES IN DENSE FOG, KILLING 176 OF 200 ON BOARD, NIGERIA, 1973

AN 23 - DEADLIEST EARTHQUAKE- HENSI PROVINCE IN NORTHERN CHINA, N ESTIMATED 830,000 KILLED, 1556

JAN 24 - TED BUNDY EXECUTED IN "OLD SPARKY", STARKE FL, 1989

JAN 25 - MANSON CHICKS LESLIE VAN HOUTEN, PATRICIA KRENWINKEL & SUSAN ATKINS FOUND GUILTY OF MUR- DER IN THE TATE/LaBIANCA CASE

JAN 26 - 2 THIGHS, AN ARM, AND THE LOWER TORSO OF A PROSTITUTE FOUND IN A BASKET IN AN ALLEY, 3rd OF 12 VICTIMS OF THE NEVER APPREHENDED CLEVELAND BUTCHER, 1936

AN 27 - VAMPIRE OF SACRAMENTO ICHARD CHASE KILLS A FAMILY OF 4, VISCERATES 1 WOMAN AND DRINKS ER BLOOD FROM A COFFEE CUP, 1978

JAN 28 - 16 YR OLD JOHN JAYNE, UPSET OVER A SPANKING, KILLS HIS FAMILY AND DOG WITH A SHOTGUN, MORAVIA, N.Y 1959

JAN 29 - 1 DRIVER AND 3 SPECTATORS ARE KILLED IN TWO SEPERATE ACCIDENTS AT THE GRAN PREMIO INT'L RACE IN ARGENTINA, 1967

JAN 31 - TED BUNDY KIDNAPS HIS FIRST VICTIM, A 21 YR OLD COED HE WILL LATER KILL OUTSIDE SEATTLE, 1974

Y'KNOW... I COULD GET TO LIKE THIS.

"WHAT'S ONE MORE PERSON ON THE FACE OF THIS EARTH, ANYWAY?" - Ted Bundy

I WAS AN ADDICT, A FIEND, A DROOLING FANATIC TRAPPED BY URGES BEYOND MY UNDERSTANDIN
I HAD A SICKNESS, A THIRST THAT COULD NOT BE SATISFIED, BUT INSTEAD CRIED OUT FOR MORE, MORE, MORE
PITY ME! I WAS--
..THE SODA THIEF!
NECTAR OF THE GODS
AMBROSIA
12 FL OZ
NK
ELIXIR
IN CANS
IT WAS THE LATE 70's, AND I WAS THIRTEEN YEARS OLD. ACCORDING TO JEWISH TRADITION, THE TORAH, AND THE RABBIS MY MOTHER WAS PAYING--I WAS NOW A MAN.
13=MAN
B-BOR-UCCH A-TOY ELL-OH-HAY-NOO...
MY GOD! WHAT AM I SAYING?!
AND WHERE'S MY MONEY?
AND LIKE ALL JEWISH MEN, I SOON LEFT MY HOME.
FOR SUMMER CAMP.
DEAR MOM- I WANT TO GO HOME!
evan Bunk 13
99 BOTTLES OF BEER ON THE WALL, 99 BOTTLES
THERE I WAS FREE TO PURSUE MY MANY MANLY INTERESTS:
SUCH AS ART...
WELL, IT WAS GONNA BE THE SUPER-ADAPTOID VERSUS SPIDER-MAN AND THE AVENGERS AND THE DEFENDERS AND THE CHAMPIONS, BUT THE SPIDER-MAN I HAD WAS BY GIL KANE AND HE'S TOO HARD TO COPY SO I COPIED A SAL BUSCEMA* MARVEL TEAM-UP AND THEN I COULDN'T FIND ANY PICTURES OF SUB-MARINER** SO I WENT SWIMMING INSTEAD.
HULK SMASH
*PRONOUNCED: "BOO-SKEE-MAH"
**PRONOUNCED "SUB-MA-REEN-ER"
...MUSIC...
IF YOU PLAY THAT @#%?! "GREASE" SOUNDTRACK ONE MORE TIME I SWEAR I'M GONNA BREAK THIS @#%?!! ALUMINUM BAT OVER YOUR HEADS!!
GREASE IS THE WAY WE ARE FEELING--
...AND LITERATURE.
HA HAHA!
"PING PONG"!
HA HA!
MAD SUPER-SPECIAL REPRINTS
PING PONG
DORKIN! SHUT UP AND GO TO BED!

I ALSO TRIED TO COURT THE OPPOSITE SEX-- BUT THE LESS WRITTEN AND DRAWN ABOUT THAT THE BETTER.
UH, WELL, Y'SEE, I REALLY, REALLY L-LIKE YOU AND UH, I WAS WONDERING IF YOU'D, YOU KNOW, WANT TO G-GO OUT W-WITH ME?
KAREN KIKTA-WHOM I'D HAD A CRUSH ON FOR THREE SUMMERS
NO.
A-ARE YOU SURE?
YES.
JETHRO TULL
SNAP!*
*SOUND OF JEWISH "MAN'S" HEART BREAKING
BUT THESE TRIVIAL DIVERSIONS PALED IN COMPARISON WITH THE ONE OBSESSION THAT TRULY RULED MY NEW, ADULT LIFE-- MY WILD, UNCONTROLLABLE THIRST FOR SODA!
SODA
Always Good
AND I'M NOT TALKING MERELY ABOUT COKE AND PEPSI HERE! NO, YOU SEE, AS A KIDHOOD CONNOISSEUR OF ALL THINGS CARBONATED AND CANNED, MY NEEDS WENT FAR BEYOND THE COLA FAMILY, EMBRACING THE ENTIRE SPECTRUM OF ARTIFICIAL FLAVORS-- SUCH AS THE EFFERVESCENT LIFT OF SEVEN-UP!
THE MATURE, LILTING BITE OF GINGER ALE!
evan
THE SHARP, HEADY ALLURE OF ROOT BEER!
evan
DRINK ME
THE SMOOTH RICHNESS OF CREAM SODA!
THE SWEET, CITRIC BLAST OF ORANGE SODA!
evan
THE MUSCULAR ATTACK OF GRAPE SODA!
THE NEAR-MEDICINAL OOMPH OF DR. PEPPER!
EVEN THE IMPROBABLE, EXOTIC SEDUCTION OF PINEAPPLE SODA!
THERE WERE ONLY TWO FLAVORS THAT EVEN I, IN THE THROES OF MY MOST FRENZIED SODA LUST COULD NOT IMBIBE:
NO!
CEL-RAY SODA! THE REFRESHMENT OF LUNATICS!
AND MANHATTAN SPECIAL COFFEE SODA! THE BLACK TAR HEROIN OF SOFT DRINKS!
NO!
evan
BUT FOR THE SODA I DID DRINK, I WOULD DO ANYTHING. I GAMBLED AT BACKGAMMON AND CARDS, TAKING MY SAP BUNKMATES' DIMES AND QUARTERS TO MY DEALER.
Coca-Cola
here's the real thing
NO MOUNTAIN DEW?! I THOUGHT YOU WERE HOLDING!
BAM!
BUT IT WAS NEVER ENOUGH! EVENTUALLY I BEGAN TO STEAL TO SATISFY MY HABIT-- AND SOON CAMP LOUEMMA WAS HAUNTED BY THE MYSTERIOUS AND OBNOXIOUS FIGURE KNOWN AS
--THE SODA THIEF!
KISS
WHO THE #©?! STOLE MY SHASTA?
SOMEONE FINISHED MY DR. BROWN'S BLACK CHERRY WHILE I WAS ON THE CAN!
GEE, SCOTT, THAT'S A DURNED SHAME. I WONDER WHO DID IT?
GURGLE
*ACTUALLY, I CAN'T WHISTLE -ev
I CAN'T EXPLAIN WHY I TURNED TO A LIFE OF CRIME. WAS IT THE THRILL OF THE GAME, OR SOMETHING IN THE SODA ITSELF?
SOMEBODY STOLE MY MOUNTAIN DEW!
HA HA HA HA HA HA
I NEVER ONCE CONSIDERED THE HEALTH RISKS--WHAT WAS I THINKING, WITH ALL THOSE NASTY KIDDIE MOUTHS CARRYING GERMS, MONO AND GOD KNOWS WHAT ELSE?
WHEN I GOT UP TO BAT I HAD HALF A RC COLA LEFT --BUT NOW IT'S ALL GONE!
I TURN AWAY FOR A MINUTE AND SOME JERK DRINKS MY MR. PIBB! ALL I GOT WAS A SIP!
BUT A SODA THIEF DOESN'T WORRY ABOUT SUCH TRIVIALITIES--ALL HE THINKS ABOUT IS THE SODA.

AND THAT'S ALL I WAS THINKING ABOUT THAT ONE FATEFUL AFTER-NOON WHEN I SPOTTED MY LATEST TWELVE OUNCE TARGET.
!
7UP
A LONE CAN OF SEVEN-UP.
evan
UNCHAPERONED AND READY FOR THE TAKING.

I SEIZED THE OPPORTUNITY --ALONG WITH THE ALUMINUM CAN-- READY TO TOSS BACK A LIFE-SUSTAINING SLUG OF NECTAROUS LIQUID...
HEH HEH HEH
♫

IMMEDIATELY, I SENSED SOMETHING WAS WRONG. THE CAN WAS THE FIRST TIP-OFF--IT WAS WARM. ALMOST HOT TO THE TOUCH!
?
* SPIDER SENSE TINGLING

BUT THE TACTILE WARNIN FROM MY FINGERS TO MY BRAIN CAME TOO LATE! I ALREADY HAD MORE THAN HALF THE CAN'S CONTENTS IN MY MOUTH!
? ! ! ?
AND WHAT I'D EXPECTED WOULD BE COOL, REFRESH ING LIQUID WAS INSTEAD A WARM, LUMPY BALL OF SICKENINGLY-SWEET MUD

GAGGING, I SPIT THE MUD BALL OUT ONTO THE FLOOR.
BLUGH!

AND TO MY HORROR THE DARK, WET PILE, LOOKING LIKE A FAT LUMP OF CHEAP CAVIAR --BEGAN TO WRIGGLE!

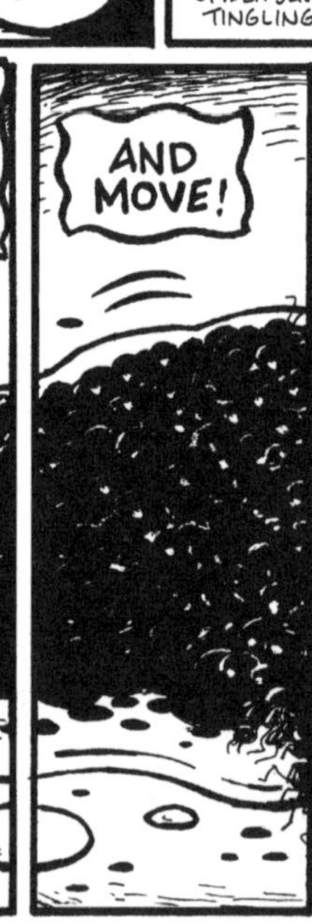

AND MOVE!

UNTIL THE MOUND OF MUD BROKE APART, REVEALING ITSELF TO BE DOZENS OF BLACK, WET, SHINY, SCATTERING ANTS!
?

THEY'D OBVIOUSLY CRAWLED INTO THE CAN HOURS EARLIER, PERHAPS EVEN AS LONG AS A DAY BEFORE--SWIMMING IN THE WARM, EVAPOR-ATING SODA UNTIL I HAD SWALLOWED THEM! YES--HOT, STICKY, SYRUPY ANTS-- --AND THEY WERE IN MY MOUTH!!!
CHEWY INSECT CENTER
AS I WASHED MY MOUTH OUT FOR WHAT SEEMED LIKE HOURS, I TRIED TO CONVINCE MYSELF THAT I HADN'T SWALLOWED ANY ANTS.

I COULDN'T BE SURE, BUT THERE WAS ONE THING I WAS CERTAIN OF.

THE SODA THIEF WAS DEAD.

YEAH, I WAS CURED ALL RIGHT. BUT HAD I TRUL LEARNED ANYTHING FROM ALL THIS? TRUE, I WAS NO LONGER THE SODA THIEF, BUT SCANT MONTHS LATE I WAS SHOPLIFTING COMIC BOOKS AND STAR WARS ACTION FIGURES FROM THE AISLES OF K-MART AND WOOLWORTH

I WAS NOW A "THIEF" THIEF.

HEY, YOU!

STAR WARS

WHOOPS!

BUT THAT'S ANOTHER STORY.

evan-∞

HEY, EVERYBODY, COME GATHER AROUND! WE'D LIKE YOU TO MEET THE NEW FOLKS IN TOWN!
THEIR NAME'S THE RILEYS AND IT'S EASY TO SAY-- THEY'RE A TIGHT-KNIT BUNCH IN WORK, REST AND PLAY!
SO LET'S ALL KILL SOME TIME, WHILE the RILEYS KILL SOME FOLKS JUST TRY TO NOT DIE LAUGHING FROM THIS BROOD'S KILLER JOKES!
PIKAC
#25
TAXIDERMY
FUN WITH FORENSICS
HUNTING HUMANS
QUICK LIME
HEY! THEY'RE THE--
MUR-DER-FA-MI-LY!
in stereo sound... where available
TONIGHT'S EPISODE-
"APRIL FUNERAL'S DAY!"
"THE MURDER FAMILY WAS FILMED BEFORE A LIVE AUDIENCE..."
CLAP CLAP CLAP CLAP CLAP CLAP CLAP CLAP CLAP
--AND SO, IN CONCLUSION, WE FEEL- AS TWO RED-HOT BLOODED AMERICAN MALES- THAT IT'S HIGH TIME FOR A POST-MORTEM PLAY-MATE--
WHISTLE
RUJER
MORNIN', DOUGLAS, ARNOLD! WHAT ARE YOU TWO HELLIONS UP TO TODAY?
UHH, NOTHIN', HARL! WE'RE, UH, JUST, UH, WRITING A "LETTER TO THE EDITOR"!
Y-YEAH! WE WANT PLAYBOY TO RUN A CENTER-FOLD OF A REAL-LIFE NAKED DEAD GIRL! AHUH-HEH-HEH!
TCH! IXNAY, ARNIE, YOU LUMMOX!
HA HA
AW, DON'T WORRY NONE BOYS! I WON'T SQUEAL TO YOUR FOLKS YOU BEEN SHOPLIFTIN' PORNO AGAIN!
HA HA
HEY! WE DIDN'T BOOST THE WHACKIN' MATERIAL! WE GOT IT FROM MOM'S DRESSER!
HA HA HA HA
PLAYBOY
SOLDIER of FORTUNE
RUJE
HA HA
Y-YEAH! WE FOUND IT WHEN WE WAS LOOKIN' FOR HER SUBSCRIPTION COPY OF SOLDIER OF FORTUNE!

SO, "DEAD PET OF THE MONTH", EH? IT IS AN IDEA AT THAT. NOTHIN'S QUITE SO "AU NATURAL" AS A NUDE IN REPOSE...
AN A NUDE DON'T NEVER GET MORE REPOSED THAN DAID!
HA HA HA
HA HA
=AHUH= AN' YOU SHOULD KNOW, HARL!

YES, I MUST SAY, SOME OF THE FINEST EXAMPLES OF THE FEMALE FORM I EVER DID SEE WAS A'LAYIN NEKKID AN' COLD ON A TEXAS MORGUE SLAB!
=SNIF= I SURELY DO AT TIMES MISS THE OL' JOB SOMETHIN' FIERCE...
HA HA HA HA

ONE SUGGESTION, BOYS - I'D SEN THAT LETTER TO HUSTLER 'STEAD OF PLAYBOY. HEF AIN'T GOT THE STONES FER THAT KINDA MEN'S ENTERTAINMENT! AN' I'D LEAVE YER NAMES AN' ADDRESS OFF, IN CASE THEY FORWARD YER LITTLE LOVE NOTE TO THE F.B.I!
HA
HUH?

ARNIE! YOU PERSONA NON-GRATA YOU! HOW MANY TIMES HAVE I TOLD YOU? NO PAPER TRAIL! ARE YOU RETARDED OR SOMETHIN'?
YOURS TROOLY ARNIE AND DOUGIE 21 OAK ST
OHHHH, I THINK SO, DOUGIE! I SORRY!
AWW HA HA HA HA HA HA

IT'S A MIRACLE WE AIN'T ON DEATH ROW THE WAY ARN GOES ABOUT BUSINESS! JUST LAST NIGHT HE ALMOST GOT US PINCHED DURING OUR CREEPY-CRAWL PANTY RAID ON THE JOHNSON TWINS' BEDROOM!
BRUJEF
SAY! I PLUM FORGOT TO TELL YA! LAST NIGHT I SEEN OLD MAN HARGREAVES NOSIN' AROUND THE JOHNSON PLACE!

WHAT?! THE DEVIL YOU SA
OH DOUGIE, THIS IS BAD! B-A-D BAD! WE GOTTA FIX IT, DOUGIE! WE GOTTA FIX IT!!

C'MON, ARN! WE'RE GONNA HAVE A CHAT WITH OLD MAN HARGREAVES!
-- BUT HONEY BE REASONABLE! WE CAN'T JUST KILL EVERYONE IN TOWN!
HEE HEE.. HUH?

M-MAYBE WE CAN FAKE A MASS SUICIDE AND GO ON THE LAM?!
CLAP WHISTLE CLAP
CLAP CLAP
GEE WHIZ, FOLKS! WHAT'S THE BIG TO-DO?

ARNIE BROKE ALL MY CRAYONS AGAIN!
NOT NOW, GEORGINA!
L-LOOK HARLAN! THE MORNING PAPER SAYS I'M UNDER SUSPICION FOR THE OAKWOOD DINER DOUBLE SLAYING!
DAILY DISPATCH

HEE HEE HEE!
I DON'T SEE WHAT'S SO FUNNY, HARLAN! ESPECIALLY WHEN WE ALL KNOW MOTHER DID IT!
HAHAHA HA
IT'S FUNNY, 'CUZ I MADE THAT PHONY HEADLINE DOWN AT THE NOVELTY SHOP! APRIL FOOLS!
HA HA CLAP CLAP
AW, HECK! NOT AGAIN WITH THE APRIL FOOL'S NONSENSE!
YEP! AN Y'ALL FELL FO' IT LIKE A BUNCHA SEVERED HEADS! HEE HEE HAW HAW!
HARLAN! HEAD'S UP!!
ARNIE! DID YOU BREAK MY CRAYONS--
LATER FOR CRAYONS! WE GOTTA GET OLD MAN HARGREAVES OUTTA SIGHT!
WOW! HE LOOKS PRETTY DEAD!
SAY, WHAT GOES ON HERE, BOYS?! WHAT HAVE YOU DONE TO POOR OLD MR. HARGREAVES?
WE JUST WANTED TO TALK TO HIM, DAD--HONEST! BUT HE GOT ALL CRAZY LOUD ON US, AN' WHEN ARNIE TRIED TO SHUT HIM UP HE SHOOK THE OLD GEEZER SO HARD HE MADE ALL THESE CRACKING AND POPPING NOISES LIKE SOMEBODY WALKIN' ON WET BUBBLE WRAP!
WOW!
HA HA
BRUJER
HONEST, DADDY-- WE NEVER MEANT T'KILL HIM!
HIS WIFE, YEAH! BUT NEVER POOR OLD MR. HARGREAVES!
HAHAHAHA HA CLAP CLAP
HEE HEE HEEE HA HA--
WHAT'S SO DARNED HILARIOUS, HARL?
HARGREAVES WASN'T NOSIN' 'ROUND LAST NIGHT! I WAS JUST JOSHIN' YA FO' AN APRIL FOOL'S GAG! HEE HA HA!
HAHA HA
AW, NOT AGAIN! I THOUGHT YOU SWORE OFF THAT STUFF AFTER LAST YEAR'S STUNT!
OH YEAH--THAT PHONY BLACKMAIL GAG.
RUJER
I STILL FEEL KINDA SORRY FOR THAT GUY I BEAT UP. AN' TORTURED WITH PLIERS. AN' DROWNED.
HA GIGGLE HA
WELL, I'M GLAD YOU'RE LAUGHING, HARLAN! YOU DO REALIZE ANOTHER BODY COULD BRING THE LAW DOWN ON US! AND THAT NOT ONLY IS THE CRAWLSPACE FULL, BUT THE BACKYARD'S BARELY GOT ROOM FOR A PINK FLAMINGO, LET ALONE A ROTTING CORPSE!
SO I HOPE YOU'RE HAPPY WITH YOUR LITTLE JOKE, HARL!
OOOOOOOH!
=SNIF= I-I'M SORRY, EVERYONE. I PROMISE, NO MORE APRIL FOOL'S JOKES FROM HERE ON IN... =SNIF=
AWWWWWWW
"THE MURDER FAMILY WILL BE BACK AFTER THESE MESSAGES..."
CHALK

THIS IS TAWNY WILCOX WITH A CHANNEL EIGHTY-EIGHT SHOWBIZ MINUTE. TRAGEDY STRUCK AT LAST NIGHT'S ROCK AND ROLL HALL OF FAME CEREMONY, WHEN KEITH RICHARDS FELL FROM AN UPPER BALCONY ONTO ROGER McGUINN AND CHRIS HILLMAN --EFFECTIVELY KILLING TWO BYRDS WITH ONE STONE.
TAWNY WILCOX
SHOWBIZ MINUTE

WHILE IT APPEARS TO HAVE BEEN AN ACCIDENT, MANY QUESTIONS REMAIN UNANSWERED. WAS RICHARDS UNDER THE INFLUENCE? WAS HE PUSHED? AND HOW THE HELL DID THOSE NOBODY BYRDS LOSERS GET BETTER SEATS THAN KEITH RICHARDS? I MEAN, HELLO! HE'S ONLY, LIKE, A ROCK GOD, PEOPLE!
?

"IN OTHER MUSIC NEWS--THE BAN RAGE AGAINST THE MACHINE HAS ANNOUNCED THAT THEY ARE BREAKIN UP. THE HARD ROCK OUTFIT, KNOWN FOR THEIR RADICAL LEFT-WING POLI TICS, MADE THE DECISION WHEN THE REALIZED THAT THEIR RECORD LABE THEIR MANAGEMENT, THEIR TOUR SPONSORS AND THEY THEMSELVES WERE ALL PART OF "THE MACHINE
WE THOUGHT ABOUT KILLING OURSELVES, BUT LIKE, WE DON KILL, Y'KNOW? WE JUST, LIKE, RAGE!
MTV
M2
MTV.COM
VH1
"THAT'S THE LATEST SHOWBIZ NEWS. WE NOW RETURN YOU TO THE MURDER FAMILY--"

WELL, WE GOT MOST OF OLD MAN HARGREAVES SQUARED AWAY. THE REST WILL HAVE TO WAIT 'TIL NIGHTFALL!
DAMN THAT HARLAN AND HIS STUPID APRIL FOOL'S GAGS! I SWEAR, SOMETIMES HE MAKES ME SO MAD I COULD DECAPITATE HIM!
NOW, NOW DEAR. LET'S ALL JUST HOPE THIS IS THE LAST OF OUR TROUBLES--
HA HA HA HA HA HA
SOLDIER OF FORTUNE
DING-DONG!

HMMM. NOW WHO THE HELL COULD THAT BE? GEORGINA, ARE YOU EXPECTING ANY FRIENDS OVER?
NOT ME, MOM! KID LOATHE AND FEA ME, REMEMBER?
HUH. LOOKS LIK A PLAINCLOTHE COP. BUT I DON'T RECOGNIZE HIM FROM THE PRECIN

HOLD ON A SECOND--WHAT IF THIS IS JUST ANOTHER OF HARLAN'S APRIL FOOL'S TRICKS?
HEY! I BET YOU'RE RIGHT! IT'S TOO SOON FOR A MISSING PERSONS CASE TO KICK IN ON HARGREAVES! SO WHAT DO WE DO?
WE DO WHAT WE HAVE TO DO. HARLAN'S GONE TOO FAR THIS TIME--INVOLVING OTHERS IN OUR AFFAIRS JUST TO PLAY A FOOL TRICK!

GEORGINA, HONEY--YOU KNOW WHAT TO DO. WE'LL BE RIGHT HERE, SO DON'T BE NERVOUS. IT'S JUST LIKE THE TIME WITH THE JEHOVAH'S WITNESS!
I'M FINE, MOM! NERVES OF STEEL!
HA HA HA
SNIF THAT'S MY BABY!

HELLO, LITTLE GIRL. MY NAME IS DETECTIV RITT. ARE YOUR FOLKS HOME? I'D LIKE TO ASK THEM A FEW QUESTIONS ABOUT YOUR NEIGHBOR, JEREMIAH HARGREAVES.
SURE COME IN "DETECT RITT

MOM! DAD! SOME-ONE HERE TO SEE YOU!
OH.. GOOD GOD..
YEEAARGH!
UF!
SHUK!
HAPPY APRIL FOOL'S DAY CHIEF!!
OH GOD OH GAAAAAHHH!
HA HA HA HA HA HA HA HA HA HA HA HA HA HA HA HA HA HA CLAP CLAP HA HA

the MURDER FAMILY

STARRED

JOHN FUCHS - MR. RILEY
MARISA SOTO - MRS RILE
PETER DONAT - DOUGIE
HUGO BUNTZ - ARNIE
DAN'LLE LEVIT - GEORGIN

AND

THURMAN MOLTING AS HARLAN KNOX

WITH

DENNIS McKAY - DETECTIV
TIM WESTON - MR. HARGREA

MAKE UP EFFECTS: ED PULASK

WRITTEN, PRODUCED AND DIRECTED BY EVAN DORK

MMI

HOUSE OF FUN PRODUCTIONS

ADVERTISING SPOKESCHARACTERS OF YESTERYEAR — WHERE ARE THEY NOW?

Admit it, you want to know, and I want to tell you, because it eats up a page of this comic.

BY EVAN DORKIN & SARAH DYER 1994

Like many former child stars, Sprout had his public battles with drugs and alcohol, leading to his 1989 appearance in the X-rated *Money Shot*. He entered rehabilitation in 1990, and is now a janitor in the Chicago public schools.

The lives of these East Coast beer mavens were markedly affected by sibling rivalry and alcoholism. The bachelor brothers fought bitterly until a drunk-driving accident killed Harry in 1979. Bert died of cirrhosis in '87.

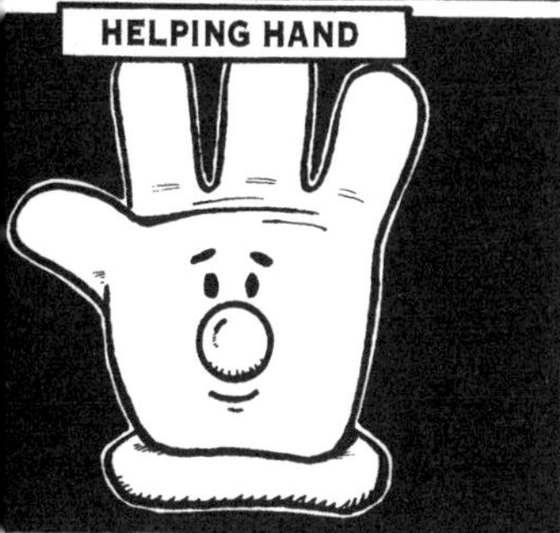

e ever-helpful extremity remained a Good maritan to the end. Known for his charity ›rk, he was tragically stabbed to death while empting to break up a fight in a Chuck E. ›eese restaurant in Lodi, N.J. in 1993.

A figure of controversy since leaving Hollywood, mostly due to alleged connections to organized crime. Indicted twice, Charlie has been acquitted each time. The Tuna lives in Boca Raton with his new nineteen-year-old bride.

Retired since the early '70s, the energetic Kilowatt is now a multi-millionaire thanks to early investment in GE. He has been happily married since 1957 to Penny-Therm, formerly of Chicago's Bastian-Blessing Utility Co.

› beloved icon was declared legally insane ›r attacking schoolchildren in 1976. After ›rs of treatment, Quisp now resides in a ›ton halfway home and has "found Jesus." ›y blame chronic LSD use for his travails.

The aggressive Punchy has been arrested on a regular basis in Hawaii and on the mainland for his assaults on vacationers. He is currently on parole for a March '94 attack in Palm Springs.

The former Hostess cake personality resides on his Arizona ranch, where he reportedly heads a quasi-religious group called Rainbow Church and has six wives. He has also reportedly amassed a "rather large gun collection."

›an "came out" in 1988 after retiring from ›mmercials to work with gay rights organi›ons. He has campaigned in Washington › spoken all over the country. His autobi›aphy, *Coming Clean*, is due out this fall.

A national tragedy. Depressed after his forced retirement in 1992, Zip entered the San Jose main post office with an AK-47. His shooting spree left seven dead and five wounded. He then turned the gun on himself.

Elsie is glue.

25¢
THE ISLAND OF MISFIT CANDY
evan-00

SOMETIME IN THE 1990'S...
HELLO, BOSS! YOU SEND FOR CHERRY CLAN?
AHEM. UH, WELL, YES. LOOK BOYS, IT'S LIKE THIS--I'M AFRAID WE'RE LETTING YOU GO.

WHAT!? YOU PINK SLIP CHERRY CLAN? BUT WHY?!

I'M SORRY BOYS, BUT YOU SEE IN TODAY'S POLITICALLY CORRECT CLIMATE "CHERRY CLAN" HAS BEEN PERCEIVED AS RACIST. SO WE HAVE DECIDED TO CHANGE THE NAME TO "CHERRY HEADS."
CHERRY HEADS

WHAT?! CHERRY CLAN NOT RACIST!!
CHERRY CLAN DELICIOUS CANDY!

I'M TRULY SORRY, BOYS, BUT MY HANDS ARE TIED. IT'S CORPORATE POLICY--WE'RE EVEN DROPPING
THE GRAPE JUST IN CASE
OH GOD =SNIF= WHY?

SHIT! WHO CARE ABOUT STUPID GRAPE?
SON OF BITCH! THIS TERRIBLE!
GODDAM SON OF BITCH LEMON HEAD..
SECURITY!

CHERRY CLAN OUT ON STREET.
CHERRY CLAN COLD.
MUST FIND WORK. MUST GO TO CANDY BOSSES!

SLAM!
SORRY! TOO RACIST!
HERSHEY'S CANDY CO.
AH!

SLAM!
CHERRY CLAN? ARE YOU KIDDIN?
NESTLE'S CANDY CO.
H!
SLAM!
I THOUGHT YOU GUYS GOT THE AXE AGES AGO!
BRACH'S CANDY CO.
AIEE!
SHIT! SON OF BITCH! EVEN BASTARD MAKING SNOT GUMMIES REFUSE CHERRY CLAN!
CHERRY CLAN OH SO WRETCHED!
WE THROW OURSELVES INTO SEA! IS OUR FATE!
HO! ICE FLOE BREAK! CHERRY CLAN SET ADRIFT!
CRAK!
IS OUR NEW FATE!
OOK! IS SLAND! HERRY LAN IS SAVED!
BUT WAIT! WHO ARE THESE PEOPLES?
GREETIN'S BROTHERS! WE'S THE CHOCOLATE BABIES!
WELCOME TO THE ISLAND OF MISFIT CANDY!!
MISFIT CANDY? PLEASE TO EXPLAIN!
SHO'! THIS HERE'S WHERE UNWANTED CANDY GOES WHEN THEY'VE BEEN DEEMED POLITICALLY IN-CO-RRECT! WE WAS DUMPED BY HEIDE BRAND FO' THEY SOLD TO HERSHEYS!
BUT INJUN ORANGE AN' CHINESE CHERRY TOOK US IN. THEY RULE THE ISLAND OF MISFIT CANDY! AN' ALL OUTCASTS IS WELCOME!
HOW!
GLEETINGS!
A-HOY! PRAISE YAHWEH! LAND T LAST! VE ARE THE GUMMY EWS! VE VERE GIVEN THE BUM'S USH VILE STEEL EEN PRODUCTION T TROLLI AND VE SEEK SANCTUARY!
OH HELL NO! NEXT THING YOU KNOW THEY'LL TAKE OVER THE WHOLE ISLAND!
UGH! BURN THEM!
ACH! VE ARE FORSAKEN! LOUSY SHVARTZERS!
HA HA HA! EVEN AMONG MISFITS YOU MISFITS!
CHERRY CLAN VERY HAPPY NOW!
EVERYONE HAPPY NOW!

Advertising Spokescharacters of Yesteryear – Where Are They Now?

Once again, we take a look at what actually became of some of America's formerly beloved commercial icons.

1. The ESSO Oildrop The Danish-born globule of petroleum literally faded from the public eye when he evaporated in 1964, paving the way for the Humble Tiger to shortly become Esso's number one spokescharacter.

2. Opie After years of beatings at the hands of the overly aggressive Punchy, Opie (also known as the "oaf" and "the tourist") successfully sued the makers of Hawaiian Punch for damages. He now resides, in failing health, in Lakeland, Florida.

3. Goofy Grape In 1980 it was revealed that the "goofy" powdered drink mix pitcher was actually suffering from ADD. Now known as "Rational Raisin", the elderly and wrinkled fruit lives in Portland, Oregon with his long time partner, Jolly Olly Orange.

4. Fruit Pie the Magician The Pie's post-Hostess magic career crumbled after a disastrous engagement at the Sands hotel in Las Vegas. Mounting debts led to the Pie's final "disappearing act" in 1990, often credited to local mobsters who held his I.O.U.s.

5. The Burger King The manic-depressive, temperamental King lost his crown after drunkenly screaming, "Your fries suck! So sayeth the King!" at BK executives during a corporate dinner. He now works as a McDonalds fry cook in Bethesda, MD.

6. Milton the Toaster Burnt out, frazzled, and forgotten, Milton was rediscovered in a Santa Monica thrift shop in 1993. Sadly, he expired during a filament replacement operation later that year, just days before he could join a speaking tour featuring former Kellogg's spokescharacters.

7. Quake The former superhero, construction worker, and cereal pitchman is now a popular motivational speaker. This fall he'll square off against his arch rival Quisp on Fox's popular Celebrity Boxing program.

8. The Humble Tiger The "Humble" Tiger was in real life an arrogant, foulmouthed egotist. Perhaps taking a cue from Esso's "put a tiger in your tank" slogan, he fathered thirty-two cubs, most illegitimate. He died unlamented in a boating accident in 1995.

9. Burt the Turtle Burt's educational films taught millions of 50's children to "duck and cover" in case of an atomic blast, but he couldn't duck skin cancer after years of on-the-job radiation exposure. After his death in 1962, his shell was put in storage at the Smithsonian.

10. The Frito Bandito The Bandito dropped out of sight after he was retired over charges of negative stereotyping. Recently he's resurfaced in the Catskills, working the stand-up circuit under his real name of Abe Lipschitz

11. Bud Man The once soaring superhero pitchman was reduced to doing personal appearances after being laid off. In 1995 he lost the right to wear the Bud Man costume after Anheuser-Busch sued him. He currently sells Amway in the midwest.

12. Mayor McCheese Details are still sketchy about the unemployment-driven "McDonaldland riots" of the mid-80's, but it is known that during the violent protest the mayor and his chief of police, Big Mac, were set upon and devoured by an angry mob of homeless Fry Guys.

13. The AMT Cool Cat The comic book spokescat for AMT model kits developed a forty-tube-a-week glue-sniffing habit that permanently damaged his brain. He now sorts glass as part of an outreach program in Rye, New York, and occasionally appears at local comic book conventions.

14. The Fruit Stripe Zebra Increasing confusion over his sexual and racial identity led the gum-selling zebra to a much-publicized nervous breakdown in 1982. She now lives happily in Atlanta, Georgia, working under the professional name of "Ms. Striped Thang".

15. Speedy Alka Seltzer Despondent over the death of Bar-B-Cutie, his wife of 32 years, Speedy committed suicide by stepping out into a heavy Chicago downpour in 2001. The rumor that his last words were "Plop, plop, fizz fizz, oh what a relief it is" remains unsubstantiated.

16. The Crunchberry Beast No one knows what has become of the Crunchberry-addicted beast since he ran away from his handlers in 1994. If you have any information as to his whereabouts, please contact this magazine c/o the address on the inside front cover.

3.
4.
7.
8.
11.
BUDWEISER
BUD
MAN
12.
15.
SPEEDY
ALKA
SELTZER
16.

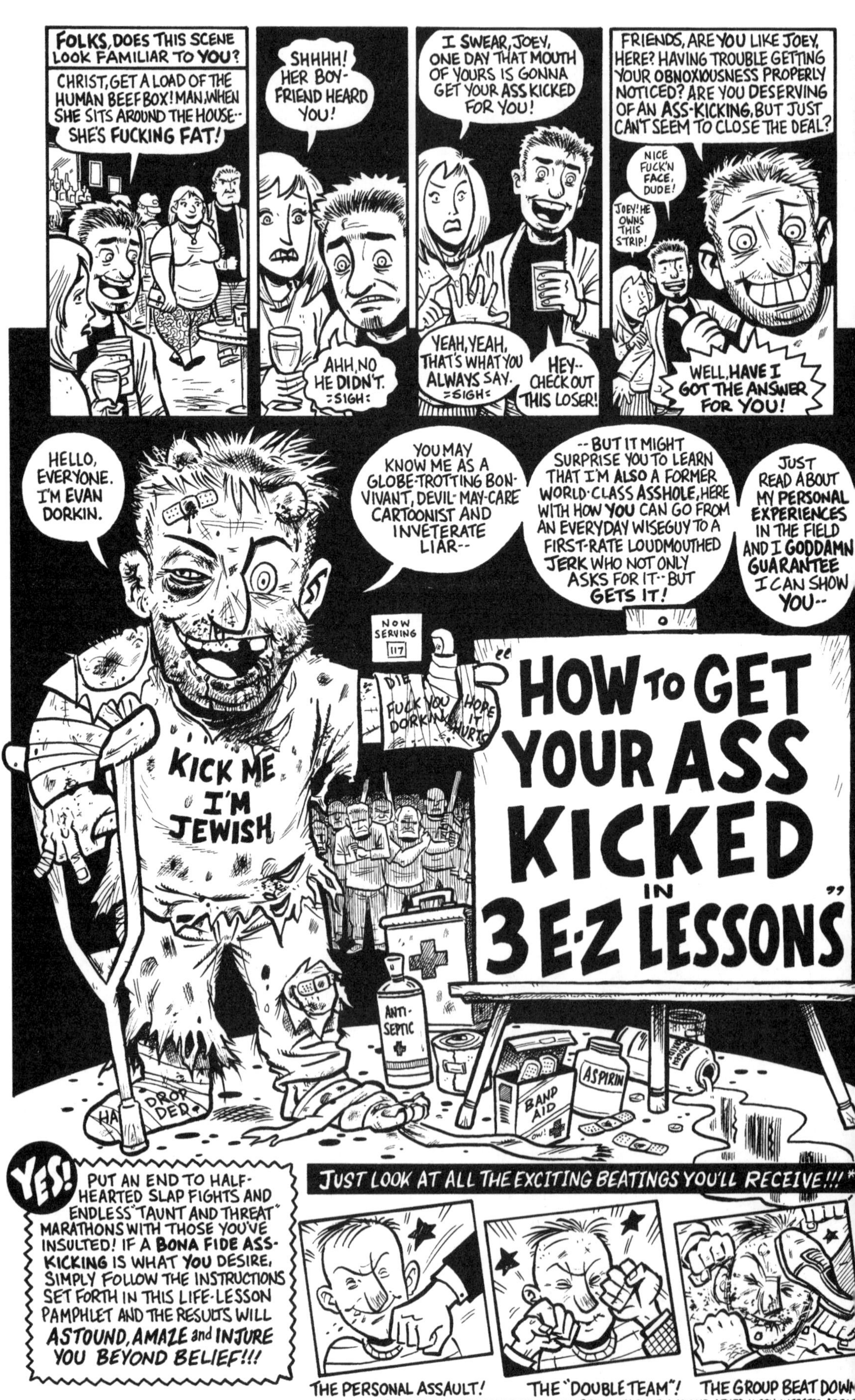
FOLKS, DOES THIS SCENE LOOK FAMILIAR TO YOU?
CHRIST, GET A LOAD OF THE HUMAN BEEF BOX! MAN, WHEN SHE SITS AROUND THE HOUSE-- SHE'S FUCKING FAT!
SHHHH! HER BOY-FRIEND HEARD YOU!
AHH, NO HE DIDN'T. =SIGH=
I SWEAR, JOEY, ONE DAY THAT MOUTH OF YOURS IS GONNA GET YOUR ASS KICKED FOR YOU!
YEAH, YEAH, THAT'S WHAT YOU ALWAYS SAY. =SIGH=
HEY-- CHECK OUT THIS LOSER!
FRIENDS, ARE YOU LIKE JOEY, HERE? HAVING TROUBLE GETTING YOUR OBNOXIOUSNESS PROPERLY NOTICED? ARE YOU DESERVING OF AN ASS-KICKING, BUT JUST CAN'T SEEM TO CLOSE THE DEAL?
NICE FUCK'N FACE, DUDE!
JOEY! HE OWNS THIS STRIP!
WELL, HAVE I GOT THE ANSWER FOR YOU!
HELLO, EVERYONE. I'M EVAN DORKIN.
YOU MAY KNOW ME AS A GLOBE-TROTTING BON-VIVANT, DEVIL-MAY-CARE CARTOONIST AND INVETERATE LIAR--
--BUT IT MIGHT SURPRISE YOU TO LEARN THAT I'M ALSO A FORMER WORLD-CLASS ASSHOLE, HERE WITH HOW YOU CAN GO FROM AN EVERYDAY WISEGUY TO A FIRST-RATE LOUDMOUTHED JERK WHO NOT ONLY ASKS FOR IT-- BUT GETS IT!
JUST READ ABOUT MY PERSONAL EXPERIENCES IN THE FIELD AND I GODDAMN GUARANTEE I CAN SHOW YOU--
NOW SERVING 117
DIE
FUCK YOU DORKIN
HOPE IT HURTS
KICK ME I'M JEWISH
"HOW TO GET YOUR ASS KICKED IN 3 E-Z LESSONS"
ANTI-SEPTIC
ASPIRIN
BAND AID
OW!
HA
DROP DEAD
YES! PUT AN END TO HALF-HEARTED SLAP FIGHTS AND ENDLESS "TAUNT AND THREAT" MARATHONS WITH THOSE YOU'VE INSULTED! IF A BONA FIDE ASS-KICKING IS WHAT YOU DESIRE, SIMPLY FOLLOW THE INSTRUCTIONS SET FORTH IN THIS LIFE-LESSON PAMPHLET AND THE RESULTS WILL ASTOUND, AMAZE and INJURE YOU BEYOND BELIEF!!!
JUST LOOK AT ALL THE EXCITING BEATINGS YOU'LL RECEIVE!!! *
THE PERSONAL ASSAULT!
THE "DOUBLE TEAM"!
THE GROUP BEAT DOWN
* RESULTS MAY BE LESS EFFECTIVE IN BERKELEY, PORTLAND AND OTHER HIPPY-INFESTED AREAS

WE'LL BEGIN WITH A LOOK AT THE BASIC EQUIPMENT YOU'LL NEED TO SUCCESSFULLY GET YOUR ASS KICKED:

FIG.1-ANATOMY OF SOMEONE WHO'S "ASKING FOR IT"

HAIR TRIGGER TEMPER
LIZARD BRAIN
BIG MOUTH
INABILITY TO NOT BLURT OUT WHAT IS ON ONE'S MIND
NASTY DISPOSITION
@☆#&!?!
INCREDIBLY FOUL VOCABULARY (LEARNED FROM HIS FUCKING MOM)
IGNORANCE (IF YOU'RE NOT SURE IF YOU'RE IGNORANT, DON'T WORRY, YOU ARE)
HIGH SARCASM QUOTIENT (NO, REALLY?)
the AMAZING SPIDER-MAN
SOFT, PINK HANDS ("CARTOONIST'S MITTS")
COMIC BOOK T-SHIRT (LIGHTNING ROD FOR POTENTIAL AGGRESSORS)
RUDE GESTURES (IMPROVISATION A PLUS)
SURPRISINGLY FAST "EMERGENCY LEGS" (IN CASE ASS-KICKING BECOMES TOO SEVERE OR IS ADMINISTERED BY HIS FUCKING MOM)
PATHETIC PHYSICAL SHAPE (PREVENTS ADEQUATE DEFENSE OR COUNTER-ATTACK)

EVAN STUART DORKIN
1976 MODEL
AGE: 11
FLATBUSH TERRACE APARTMENTS
53RD ST AND AVE H
BROOKLYN, NY

INFORMATION PROVIDED BY THE HOUSE OF FUN ©2002

F YOU ARE ONE OF THE UCKY ONES WHO HAS THE PROPER BODY TYPE AND EGATIVE MENTAL OUT-OOK REQUIRED FOR AN ASS-KICKING-- CONGRATULATIONS! *BUT NOT SO FAST!!!*

OU'RE NOT OUT OF THE RYING PAN AND INTO THE RE YET! AS A PROSPECTIVE ELF-FULFILLING VICTIM" OU'D DO WELL TO REMEMBER THESE WORDS TO LIVE DANGEROUSLY BY:

INITIATION + IRRITATION + ESCALATION = CONFRONTATION!

INITIATION!

MAKING CONTACT WITH YOUR SOON-TO-BE AGGRESSOR(S). OFTEN TRIGGERED ACCIDENTALLY. LEARN TO RECOGNIZE AND EXPLOIT SUCH SITUATIONS!

IRRITATION!

BECOMING A MAJOR ANNOYANCE TO YOUR AGGRESSOR. REMEMBER, THE FLY IN THE OINTMENT GETS THE DOCTOR'S APPOINTMENT!

ESCALATION!

OFTEN A SINGLE IRRITATION ISN'T ENOUGH TO WARRANT A SOCK IN THE EYE. IF SO, PRESS YOUR LUCK UNTIL IT TURNS BAD, FORCING THE AGGRESSOR TO RESORT TO VIOLENCE!

WORD OF CAUTION BEFORE WE OVE ON TO OUR 3 E-Z LESSONS. HESE LESSONS DATE BACK TO Y CHILDHOOD, CIRCA 1975. HILE STILL VALID FOR BOTH HILDREN AND ADULTS SEEKING MODERN DAY ASS-KICKING, HANGES IN OUR SOCIETY INCE THAT TIME SHOULD E CAREFULLY TAKEN INTO ACCOUNT!

SO ALWAYS USE YOUR OWN JUDGEMENT AS TO WHETHER YOU ARE INSTIGATING A BEATING, RATHER THAN A STABBING, SHOOTING OR CAR DRAGGING.

WHACHOO CALL ME?
PUM PUM
HEY!
NO FAIR!

LESSON ONE

GETTING YOUR ASS KICKED BY AN INDIVIDUAL

THE SET-UP: I'M ELEVEN YEARS OLD, AND I'M COMING HOME FROM SCHOOL ON THE BUS WHEN I BUMP INTO ANOTHER KID. OR HE BUMPS INTO ME. WHATEVER.

KENT
?
INITIATION

TAKING A BRIEFCASE TO SCHOOL = BONUS NERD POINTS!

RATHER THAN LET THIS MINOR INCIDENT PASS, I START LAYING INTO THE KID WITH EVERY CURSE WORD I KNOW.

@☆#!!
HEY, LOOK--
@&!#?!
@#*%!?!!
HEY--
IRRITATION
ESCALATION

NOW, NOTICE HOW MY PERVERSE GENIUS PICKED SUCH AN UNTENABLE AND DANGEROUS LOCATION FOR THIS PARTICULAR EXERCISE:
CLOSE QUARTERS W/ NO ROOM FOR ESCAPE
NO BACK UP
SLOW BURN
CONTINUED HARANGUE
PHYSICALLY FIT TARGET
LITTLE CHANCE OF ADULT INTERFERENCE
BRIEFCASE ALLOWS ONLY ONE FREE HAND
THESE CONDITIONS ENSURED A THOROUGH ASS-KICKING IF VIOLENCE ERUPTED. AND VIOLENCE WAS ALL I COULD EXPECT AFTER I LET LOOSE WITH A BURST OF FOULMOUTHERY THAT WOULD REDDEN A TEAMSTER-
LAST STRAW
AS I'D EXPECTED, THE SAP PLAYED RIGHT INTO MY HANDS! HE SHOUTED AS HE SNAPPED OFF A VICIOUS SIDE KICK, SENDING ME INTO THE REAR EXIT WELL, KNOCKING THE AIR OUT OF ME AND SMASHING MY HEAD INTO THE DOORS...
1ST THOUGHT
HOLY SHIT! H-HE KUNG FU'D ME! AN ACTUAL ASIAN USING ACTUAL MARTIAL ARTS! JUST LIKE the EIGHTEEN BRONZEMEN!
HOLY SHIT! my-my GUTS are on FIRE!
2ND THOUGHT
I CRAWLED OFF THE BUS AT THE NEXT STOP, BEATEN, BRUISED AND BATTERED. BUT BEYOND THAT, I HAD SUCCESSFULLY GOTTEN MY ASS KICKED ON MY TERMS!
BRRM
KOFF KOFF
OOOH MY GUTS
NOW, THEN-- SEE HOW EASY THAT WAS?
LET'S MOVE ON TO OUR SECOND LESSON!
LESSON TWO
GETTING YOUR ASS KICKED BY TWO INDIVIDUALS
THE BASIC SET-UP IS SIMILAR TO THAT OF LESSON ONE. HOWEVER, HERE I UPPED THE ANTE BY INSTIGATING AN ARGUMENT WITH NOT ONE, BUT TWO POTENTIAL ASSAILANTS, BOTH OF WHOM WERE BIGGER THAN I WAS.
F-WORD S-WORD M-F-COMPOUND WORD etc etc!
IRRITATION + ESCALATION
STYX
SETTING: ROY H. MANN JUNIOR HIGH SCHOOL CAFETERIA
MY TACTIC HERE TO GOAD BOTH INDIVIDUALS WAS TO INSULT THEIR INTELLIGENCE, UTILIZING SMART-ASS TECHNIQUES, APPLIED SARCASM AND DAZZLING VULGARITY.
KRA-#✡@&!!-KOOM!
STYX
HOWEVER, I'D MADE A SERIOUS MISCALCULATION, NOT NOTICING A NEARBY TEACHER WHO PROMPTLY RUINED WHAT WAS OBVIOUSLY A ROYAL ASS-KICKING TO-BE.
YER DEAD Y'HEAR ME? DEAD!
F WORD!

NEEDN'T HAVE WORRIED. MINUTES LATER AS I WENT OUT-
IDE TO THE PLAYGROUND, THE TWO KIDS APPEARED FROM
ITHER SIDE OF ME. BEFORE I KNEW WHAT WAS HAPPENING,
NIFE-EDGE KARATE CHOPS SMASHED INTO MY NECK AND THROAT.

TO THIS DAY IT'S THE ONLY TIME I'VE EVER BLACKED OUT WITHOUT THE AID OF ALCOHOL. I AWOKE SOON AFTER TO SEE PEOPLE STANDING OVER ME LIKE I WAS THE DEAD GUY IN THAT JOHNNY CRAIG EC STORY. (VAULT OF HORROR #34, DEC '54)

OKAY, NOW I KNOW WHAT YOU'RE THINKING.

PSHH! ANYONE CAN GET THEIR ASS KICKED BY ONE OR TWO PEOPLE! BUT HOW ABOUT A WHOLE BUNCH OF PEOPLE?!
JOEY!

WHICH BRINGS US TO LESSON THREE.

LESSON THREE

GETTING YOUR ASS KICKED BY A GROUP

ODDLY ENOUGH, THIS EXAMPLE ALSO INVOLVES A BUS. HOWEVER, IT WAS NO MERE "ONE AND DONE" BIT. THIS SITUATION REQUIRED A SUBTLE APPROACH IN ORDER TO MOTIVATE THOSE KIDS BEHIND ME TO KICK THE LIVING **SHIT OUT OF ME**!

THIS WAS THE COOL CROWD, THE BACK-OF-THE-BUS CROWD, THE CROWD THAT LAUGHED LOUDLY AND SMOKED AND INTIMIDATED THE OTHER KIDS. THE CROWD THAT HAD GIRLS IN IT.

ORDING OVER THEM WAS THE **BIG DUMB** CARY KID. YOU KNOW, THE **GIANT MONSTER** ID THAT GOT **LEFT BACK** TEN OR TWELVE IMES AND BULLIED ALL THE UNCOOL KIDS.

NCOOL KIDS IKE **ME**.

I WAS IN TERRIFIED AWE OF THE BACK-OF-THE-BUS-CROWD. I'D STARE AT THEM EVERY SCHOOL DAY AND WONDER WHAT IT WAS LIKE TO BE A DUMB DEFIANT COOL KID SITTING IN THE BACK OF THE BUS WITH GIRLS.

ANYWAY, ONE FATEFUL DAY THE BIG DUMB SCARY KID STOLE THE REAR EXIT MIRROR.

AHUH! HUH!

I DON'T KNOW **WHY** HE DID IT, BUT AS THE SCHOOL'S BIG DUMB SCARY KID HE WAS **ENTITLED** TO DO BIG, DUMB SCARY THINGS.

HEN THE DRIVER OTICED THAT THE IRROR WAS MISSING, E STOPPED THE BUS, ALKED INTO THE ACK AND SAID, OKAY, WHO TOOK THE MIRROR?" O ONE SAID A ORD--BUT I AW A GOLDEN PPORTUNITY...

HEY!
I KNOW WHO DID IT!

INITIATION!

THE BUS WENT QUIET. EVERYONE WAITED FOR ME TO RAT, BUT I DIDN'T JUST WANT THE BIG DUMB SCARY KID PISSED AT ME. I WANTED THE WHOLE CROWD.
SO IN A NUANCED BUT LUNATIC MOVE, I DECIDED TO SHOW UP THE DRIVER AND GIVE HIM THE AIR IN A PATHETIC BID TO SHOW THE OTHERS I WAS "COOL".
BUT I'M NOT GONNA TELL YOU!
HA! HA!
FRUSTRATED BY MY PLOY, THE DRIVER WENT BACK TO HIS SEAT AND STARTED THE BUS. THAT'S WHEN THE BIG DUMB SCARY GUY GRABBED ME.
THE LOOK IN HIS EYES SUGGESTED THAT I WAS FAR FROM COOL. THE PUNCH IN THE FACE CONFIRMED THIS FACT.
THE BIG DUMB SCARY KID THEN THREW ME TO THE BACK OF THE BUS LIKE I WAS A SLAB OF PORK LOIN TOSSED TO A PACK OF WILD, HUNGRY DOGS.
AS IF ON CUE, THE ENTIRE HORDE PROCEEDED TO KICK, PUNCH AND STOMP THE LIVING BEJEESUS OUT OF ME.
IT WAS MORE THAN I COULD HANDLE. AFTER AN ETERNITY PASSED I WAS TOSSED AT THE FEET OF THIS CUTE GIRL, AND I REMEMBER THINKING...
OH, THANK GOD! SHE WON'T HURT ME... SHE'S A CUTE GIRL!
THE CUTE GIRL LIFTED HER FOOT AND KICKED ME HARD, RIGHT IN THE KISSER.
AND I WAS GIVEN ANOTHER REASON TO QUESTION THE EXISTENCE OF GOD.
AFTER A FEW MORE ROUNDS OF HUMAN HACKY-SACK, I WAS THROWN OFF THE BUS, BEATEN, BRUISED AND BLEEDING. (WITH A LENGTHY WALK HOME, TO BOOT.)
BY INCITING MOB VIOLENCE, I HAD REACHED THE PINNACLE OF MY CAREER. THERE WAS NOWHERE ELSE TO GO.
SO I RETIRED. SURE, I'VE SINCE BEEN INVOLVED IN A FEW FIGHTS, A BAR BRAWL OR TWO, AND A PARKING LOT MELEE WHICH LED ME TO ALMOST STAB SOMEONE... BUT THAT RANDOM JAZZ COULD HAPPEN TO ANYBODY! IT'S DIFFERENT WHEN YOU ASK FOR IT!
I KNOW THIS DIFFERENCE, AND NOW SO DO YOU! SO GET OUT THERE AND SEE WHAT KIND OF BLOODSHED YOUR BURGEONING OBNOXIOUS PERSONALITY CAN BRING ABOUT! START SLOW WITH CHILDREN OR THE HANDICAPPED, THEN WORK YOUR WAY UP TO THE ASS-KICKING YOU KNOW YOU DESERVE
IT WORKED FOR ME! :OOF:
OH, JOEY!
WE HOPE YOU'VE ENJOYED THIS PAMPHLET!
LOOK FOR THESE OTHER FINE EVAN DORKIN LIFE STUDY PUBLICATIONS AT A THRIFT SHOP OR TRASH BIN NEAR YOU!
© 2002 EVAN DORKIN -
HOW TO GET YOUR ASS KICKED IN 2 E-Z LESSONS (ADVANCED STUDY FOR AGES 18-23)
K-CHING!
BOUNCER
HOW TO GET FIRED FROM A COMIC SHOP IN 10 E-Z LESSONS
I ONLY HIT THE KID ONCE!
HOW TO BOTCH A FOURSOME IN 1 PAINFUL LESSON
:GULP: SAY, IS THAT THE TIME?
SORRY, "HOW TO DO NOTHING ALL DAY AND STILL BE A PROFESSIONAL CARTOONIST" HAS BEEN DELAYED YET AGAIN.

the INVISIBLE COLLEGE
--AND THAT, MY FRIENDS, IS HOW DEL SHANNON REALLY DIED. PITY, eh?
AND TO THINK, JUST ONE DAY LATER, HE MIGHT VERY WELL HAVE BE-COME THE NEWEST TRAVELING WILBURY. PERHAPS IT WAS FOR THE BEST.
OF SECRET KNOWLEDGE
AS RELATED TO EVAN DORKIN 02

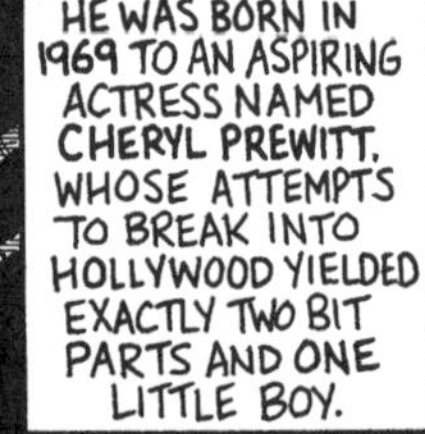

WALTER NEVER KNEW WHO HIS FATHER WAS. NEITHER DID CHERYL, ALTHOUGH SHE HAD NARROWED IT DOWN TO EITHER A KEY GRIP, A STUNT COORDINATOR, OR ONE OF SIX CASTING AGENTS SHE'D "READ FOR".

IN 1971, CHERYL LEFT TINSELTOWN FOR SAN DIEGO, WHERE SHE BEGAN DATING A COMMERCIAL PHOTOGRAPHER NAMED BOBBY RIVINGTON.

GKKB BBLBB BLLLL--

HE SPAGHETTI BABY BECAME ONE OF THE BEST-SELLING ON- CELEBRITY POSTERS OF ITS TIME, RIVALED ONLY BY THE POINTED "KISS YOUR ASS GOODBYE" ANTI-NUKE ATIRE AND THE "HANG IN THERE" KITTEN IMAGE.
DUDE... SPAGHETTI BABY.
#6
OH, MAN, THAT IS SO COOL!

CHERYL AND BOBBY, HOWEVER, SAW NO EXTRA PROFIT FROM THESE SALES. EMBITTERED, THEY ATTEMPTED TO DUPLICATE THE SUCCESS OF THE SPAGHETTI BABY ON THEIR OWN.
SAAAY...

HESE ATTEMPTS LED TO MARATHON PHOTO SHOOTS WHICH SAW WALTER COVERED IN FRUIT, VEGETABLES, RAW MEAT, EAFOOD, RICE, PEANUT BUTTER AND JELLY, CHOPSUEY, CHOW MEIN, BEANS, MOLASSES, HONEY PUDDING, ICE CREAM, ELLO, APPLESAUCE, TANDOORI CHICKEN, JERK CHICKEN, CHICKEN NOODLE SOUP, GEFILTE FISH AND OTHER FOODSTUFFS.
BAKED BEANS
ONSIDERED REVOLTING, EXPLOITATIVE AND UNCOMMERCIAL, NONE OF THE PHOTOGRAPHS WERE EVER BOUGHT.

N A TIP FROM A FORMER CLIENT, THE OLICE RAIDED BOBBY'S STUDIO. WALTER VAS TAKEN AWAY FROM HIS MOTHER AND PLACED INTO FOSTER CARE.
DON'T TAKE HIM! DON'T TAKE MY SPAGHETTI BAAABYYY
THOUGH CHILD ABUSE CHARGES WERE OPPED, WALTER NEVER SAW HER AGAIN.

SHE LEFT HER LITTLE SPAGHETTI BABY ALONE TO COPE WITH A LIFELONG FOOD PHOBIA, EATING DISORDERS, AND THE RECURRING NIGHTMARE THAT HE WAS DROWNING IN TOMATO SAUCE.
WELL, THAT WAS CERTAINLY DEPRESSING. HOW ABOUT SOMETHING A LITTLE MORE -- UPLIFTING, OLD MAN?
AN IRONIC CHOICE OF WORDS, SIR. FOR IT JUST SO HAPPENS MY NEXT TALE IS THAT OF THE GREAT MACY'S BALLOON HUNT OF 1932.

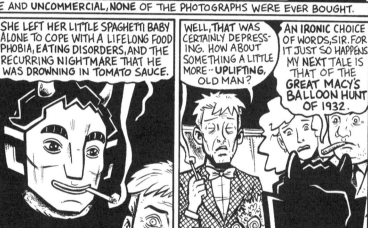

YOU ALL KNOW ABOUT THE MACY'S THANKSGIVING DAY PARADE, BUT DID YOU KNOW THAT IN 1928, MACY'S BEGAN TO MARK THE END OF THE EVENT BY RELEASING THE BALLOONS?
INDEED, THEY EVEN OFFERED A REWARD FOR THE RETURN OF THE DEFLATED HIDES, THE BOUNTY DETERMINED BY THE SIZE OF THE BALLOON.

THE FOLLOWING NOVEMBER SAW A MASSIVE TURNOUT FOR THE EVENT, AS MANY HIT HARD BY THE DEPRESSION SAW THE HUNT AS THEIR ONLY MEANS TO SOME CASH.
GANGWAY! 'DAT DRAGON'S MINE!
LIKE HELL IT IS!!
BACK OFF ALLA' YOUSE! I SAW HIM FOIST!
IN 1931 A THRILL-SEEKING AVIATOR SNAGGED THE PIG BALLOO
IN THE SKIES ABOVE BROOKLYN, NEARLY CAUSING HUNTERS
BELOW TO RIOT. AND A BRAWL OVER ANDY THE ALLIGATOR
RESULTED IN HIS BEING RETURNED IN SEVERAL PIECES
WHADDAYA MEAN, NO REWARD?!?
HOWEVER, THESE INCIDENTS
PALED IN COMPARISON TO THE
FOLLOWING YEAR'S DEBACLE

THE 1932 RELEASE WENT BADLY FROM THE START, AS DESPERATE BOUNTY HUNTERS GRABBED ONTO THE ROPES OF THE LARGEST BALLOON--

--THE KATZENJAMMER KID NAMED FRITZ.

THEIR PLAN WAS TO HANG ONTO THE BALLOON UNTIL IT RAN OUT OF HELIUM AND GENTLY LANDED.

IT DID NOT BEAR FRUIT.

TWO OF THE MEN IMMEDIATELY WENT CRA
ING INTO THE WINDOWS OF A NEARBY HOTEL-

--WHILE THE REST QUICKLY LOST THEIR GRI
AND PLUMMETED TO THE GROUND. ONE MA
DIED IN THE FALL. THE OTHERS WISHED THEY HA

THE OTHER BALLOON HUNTERS --ON FOOT, BY CAR, AND EVEN ON HORSEBACK--DOGGEDLY PURSUED FRITZ ONE HUNDRED MILES INTO NEW JERSEY, LEAVING A NUMBER OF ROAD ACCIDENTS, TRAFFIC JAMS AND FIST FIGHTS IN THEIR WAKE.

EVENTUALLY THE DEFLATING DIRIGIBLE DESCENDED UPON A FIELD, WHERE HE WAS MET BY SCORES OF RIFLE AND SHOTGUN-TOTING BIG GAME HUNTERS, ALL HOPING TO BAG THE TEUTONIC TOT.

NEVITABLY, ARGUMENTS BROKE OUT OVER THE DRIFTING JACKPOT.
HE'S OURS I TELLYA! WE BEEN OLLIN' DAT KATZENBASTID ALLA' AY FROM FITTY-FIT STREET!
WELL I SAYS I GOTS THE RIGHT T'SHOOT ANY FAT FLOATIN' KRAUT BOY COMES ON M'LAND! ANNA SAME GOES FER' TRESPASSIN' NEW YORK CITY BOYS, TOO!
WHEN SOMEONE FINALLY SHOT AT THE PRIZE, IT TRIGGERED A GUN BATTLE AMONGST THE HUNTERS, WHO ALL BELIEVED THAT THEY'D BEEN FIRED UPON.
CRAK
PUM
CRAK
CRAK
CRAK
THE MELEE CONTINUED BENEATH THE ALLEN GOODYEAR CARCASS, ENDING ONLY WHEN THE LOCAL AUTHORITIES ARRIVED TO BREAK IT UP.
CONGRATULATIONS! YOU HAVE FOUND "FRITZ"! PLEASE RETURN THE LITTLE SCAMP TO US AT MACY'S 34th ST. AND BROADWAY, N.Y. TO COLLECT YOUR REWARD - HAPPY THANKSGIVING, 1932 -
IN THE END TWENTY-THREE MEN WERE INJURED, THREE OF THEM FATALLY. AS FOR FRITZ, HE TOO WAS A CASUALTY, HAVING BEEN SHREDDED IN THE FRACAS.
MACY'S HUSHED UP THE SORRY AFFAIR WITH THEIR CHECKBOOK, AND THEREAFTER ABANDONED THE ANNUAL BALLOON RELEASE.
GEE, I STILL CAN'T GET OVER THAT POOR SPAGHETTI BABY. IF HE WAS MY KID--
OH, NOW STOP IT, WILL YA?
NOW, THEN, IF SOMEONE WOULD BE SO KIND AS TO ORDER ANOTHER ROUND, I'LL REWARD YOU WITH THE BRIEF CAREER OF THE WORLD'S FIRST AND ONLY RODEO MIME.
IT'S A DEAL!
AH, TEDDY! PERFECT TIMING, OLD BOY.
I'LL HAVE ANOTHER ROB ROY, AND--
SAY, YOU'RE NOT OUR WAITER--
OH, GOOD GOD.
NO, I'M NOT YOUR WAITER.
BUT I'VE WAITED FIVE YEARS TO GET EVEN WITH THAT UNHOLY PIECE OF PLASTIC.

HELLO, DAVID. I'VE BEEN EXPECTING YOU.
ERR-- SHOULDN'T SOMEONE CALL THE POLICE?
NO NEED. MY FRIEND HERE MAY BE ARMED, UNSTABLE, AND APPARENTLY STEWED TO THE GILLS... BUT HE'LL CAUSE NO HARM.
MATCH ME, SIDNEY.
HUH-Y-YOU THINK YOU KNOW EVERY-THING, DON'T YOU?
T-CLIK
AS A MATTER OF FACT, I DO. JUST AS I KNOW YOU'RE HERE TO GIVE ME SOMETHING. RIGHT, DAVID?
G-GIVE YOU--?! WHA LEFT TO GIVE, YO SON OF A BITCH EVERYTHING I HA IS GONE! MY WIF MY FAMILY, M-M HEALTH--

AND YOU RECEIVED NOTHING IN RETURN? LET'S NOT BE SO DISINGENUOUS, MY BOY. I GAVE YOU SOMETHING FAR GREATER THAN MERE FLESH OR KIN!
I GAVE YOU KNOWLEDGE.
S-SOME THINGS A MAN SHOULDN'T KNOW...
YES, AND NOW YOU KNOW THAT, TOO. SO LET'S NOT BE SO BITTER. REMEMBER, I DIDN'T CRAWL ONTO YOUR HAND LIKE SOME PARASITE. YOU PUT ME THERE--
ALL RIGHT!
SO WHAT IF I DID?! WHAT DO YOU WANT FROM ME?!
ONLY THAT WHICH DOESN'T BELONG TO YOU. THAT IS WHY YOU'RE HERE, ISN'T IT? TO UNBURDEN YOURSELF?
AND WHAT DOE THAT GET ME THA I WOULDN'T GET IF I PUT SIX BULLETS INTO YO AND YOUR JUICE SUPPLY THERE

THANK YOU, DAVID.
AND, GOOD-BYE.
HA HA! YEAH, OKAY! ADIOS TO YOU TOO, PAL!
DO NOT BEND
YOU AND YOUR NEW COW!
YOU POOR BASTARD. YOU DON'T GET IT, DO YOU?
HE'S NOT THE PUPPET. YOU ARE.
YOU ALL ARE!
BUT NOT ME!
NOT ANYMORE! HA HAAA!!
HAT'S A REAL CRYIN' SHAME THAT WALKED OUTTA HERE.
MORE THAN YOU KNOW.
SCREEEEEE
WHUMP
SPASH
HEY! SOMEONE CALL 911! THAT NUT JUST GOT CREAMED BY A TRUCK!
OPEN THIS FOR ME, WILL YOU, BRETT?
DO NOT BEND
HAT'S WHAT THIS WAS ALL ABOUT? OME RIPPED UP OLD PAPER?
NADINE!
THIS "RIPPED UP OLD PAPER", MY DEAR, IS ALL THAT REMAINS OF A COMIC BOOK STORY WRITTEN BY A MAN NAMED DR. FREDRIC WERTHAM.
meet FATHER TIME AND THAT BOY DYNAMO--- THE CLOCK KID
1941
THAT FOR YOU--- HA-HA-HA
WHO?
HUH. NEVER HEARD OF HIM.
AND WHY WOULD YOU HAVE? WERTHAM WAS THE SENIOR PSYCHIATRIST FOR THE NEW YORK DEPARTMENT OF HOSPITALS FROM 1932 TO 1952.
BUT HE IS BETTER KNOWN TO A DWINDLING NUMBER OF AMERICAN COMIC BOOK ENTHUSIASTS AS THE BOOGEYMAN WHOSE CRUSADE AGAINST COMICS DEVASTATED THE MEDIUM IN THE 1950'S.
LITTLE DO THEY KNOW THE TRUE REASON FOR HIS HATRED OF COMICS.

WERTHAM, A GERMAN IMMIGRANT, FIRST ENCOUNTERED COMICS IN AMERICAN NEWSPAPERS, USING THE "SIMPLE" STRIPS TO HELP HIM IMPROVE HIS READING SKILLS.

"DAG--DAG-NAB DOT KOP. I VISH HE'D GO AVAY SO I CAN--CREASE DOT KAT'S NOODLE." HEH HEH-- DOT IGNATZ.
KRAZY KAT

HE BECAME SUCH A FAN OF THE "FUNNIES" THAT HE BOUGHT SOME OF THE EARLIEST NEWSSTAND COMIC BOOKS, WHICH REPRINTED NEWSPAPER STRIPS.

ACH DU LIEBER! MUTT UND JEFF!
MALTED MILK
RADIO
THE SPIDER
BALLYHOO
JUDGE
COLLIERS
COWBOY SONGS
FAMOUS FUNNIES
CENTURY OF COMICS
SKIPPY COMICS
FAMOUS FUNNIES

AS THE DECADE PASSED, WERTHAM CON TINUED TO READ COMICS, ALBEIT IN SECRE BY 1939 HE BECAME FASCINATED WIT THE EMERGING "SUPER" HERO CHARACTER

FREDRIC?
UBERMENSCH...
SUPERMAN

--ESPECIALLY WHEN THEY BEGAN TO WAGE FOUR-COLOR **WAR ON HITLER**.

SO OBSESSED WAS HE WITH THESE COSTUMED HEROES THAT IN 1941 HE ENLISTED THE MEAGER TALENTS OF A 17-YEAR OLD LOCAL ARTIST NAMED SOLLY WEISS TO DELINEATE THE EXPLOITS OF HIS OWN CREATIONS, THE **AXIS-SMASHING**--

FATHER TIME-- AND HIS YOUNG ALLY, THE CLOCK KID!
NO, NO, IT NEEDS MORE BLUT, LIKE IN DER BLACK TERROR! GIVE DEM NAZIS VOT DEY DESERF!
BLACK TERROR
CAPTAIN AMERICA
THE SHIELD
SUPERMAN

HOWEVER, EVEN THE SHODDIEST OF PUBLISHERS DEEMED FATHER TIME TOO **BIZARRE** TO PRINT.

AN WHAT'S WIT 'DIS GRECO-ROMAN WRASSLIN' IN THE HOUR-GLASS HQ? 'DAT'S NERTZ!
BUT DEY MUST TRAIN TO KILL NAZIS, YES?
NOT LIKE DAT 'DEY DON'T! TRY CHESLER, HE'LL PRINT ANYTHING!
B-BUT HE SENT US HERE!

CRUSHED BY REJECTION, WERTHA BURNED HIS COMIC COLLECTIO TORE UP THE FATHER TIME STRI AND VOWED **REVENGE** ON THE INDUSTRY THAT SPURNED HIM

SOON I VILL BE LIKE A BLACK TERROR!
KILLINK ALL DER VERDAMMT COMICS FOR GUT!

WERTHAM'S VENDETTA BEGAN IN EARNEST IN 1948 WITH A SERIES OF LECTURES, SYMPOSIUMS AND MAGAZINE ARTICLES WARNING AMERICA OF THE "THREAT" COMIC BOOKS POSED TO THEIR CHILDREN AND THEIR NATION.

HIS INFLUENTIAL 1954 MANIFESTO, "SEDUCTION OF THE INNOCENT," BLAMED COMICS FOR A NATIONAL RISE IN **MURDER, DRUG ADDICTION**, TEENAGE PREGNANCY AND **HOMOSEXUALITY**. AT A SENATE HEARING LATER THAT YEAR, HE TESTIFIED THAT, "HITLER WAS A BEGINNER COMPARED WITH THE **COMICS** INDUSTRY." WERTHAM BELIEVED **NONE** OF THIS.

THE PUBLIC **DID**, HOWEVER--AND THE INDUSTRY WAS FORCED TO ADOPT AN EMASCULATING, SELF-CENSORING CODE IN ORDER TO SURVIVE.

ULTIMATELY, A **FRUSTRATED** WERTHAM COULDN'T KILL COMICS, BUT HE CERTAINLY HELPED CRIPPLE THEM.

IRONICALLY, WERTHAM ALSO FAILED TO DESTROY HIS **OWN COMIC**, AS SOLLY WEISS HAD RETRIEVED THE PAGES FROM THE GOOD DOCTOR'S TRASH.

EVENTUALLY, THEY CAME INTO MY POSSESSION. FIVE YEARS AGO I ENTRUSTED DAVID WEISS TO SEND THEM TO A LIBRARY IN NEW ZEALAND...
POOR DAVID. HE WAS A FINE COMPANION.

17

NOW HE'S JUST ANOTHER STORY.

AND ADIOS TO YOU, TOO ~

"FROM UNTAMED SWITZERLAND COMES UNTOLD TERROR and INCOMPREHENSIBLE PSYCHOBABBLE!"

"MIGHTY CARL JUNG"

"BEYOND YOUR WILDEST DREAMS!"

"DEFYING ALL ANALYSIS!"

VAS IST ???
THE GAS BOMBS ARE WORKING!
SLAP THEM CHAINS ON 'IM MEN! IF WE GET OUTTA THIS ALIVE WE'RE IN THE CHIPS FOR GOOD!
BANG!
AK!
FOOM!
THE KABALA
ALCHEMY
AU

HE'S ALWAYS BEEN A KING IN HIS WORLD, BUT WE'LL TAME HIM! WHY, THE WHOLE WORLD WILL PAY TO SEE HIM! WE'RE MILLIONAIRES, BOYS! I CAN SEE IT NOW-- IN A FEW MONTHS IT'LL ALL BE UP IN LIGHTS!

STRIKING! STARTLING! STAGGERING!
MIGHTY CARL JUNG
the 8TH WONDERER OF THE WORLD!!
also featuring the Nicholas Brothers • the Ray Cardona Orch.

--THANK YOU LADIES AND GENTLEMEN, FOR YOUR KIND APPLAUSE!
AND NOW THAT YOU'VE HEARD MY STORY--
STRIKING! STARTLING! STAGGERING!
MIGHTY CARL JUNG
the 8TH WONDERER OF THE WORLD!!
THE SWISS CHALET

--LET ME NOW PRESENT TO YOU THE LIVING PROOF OF OUR ADVENTURE!
THE EIGHTH WONDERER OF THE WORLD! MIGHTY-- CARL--
SWISS CHALET

--JUNG!
OOOOOOOH!
=GASP!=
=CHOKE=
AAAAAH!
=GULP=

DON'T BE ALARMED! THOSE CHAINS ARE MADE OF CHROMIUM STEEL!
WE LOST TEN MEN CAPTURING HIM! TWO MORE WENT MAD ARGUING THE MYSTICAL INTERCONNECTEDNESS OF SYNCHRONICITY WITH HIM ON THE TRIP HOME! BUT WE'RE SAFE-- SAFE TO HEAR FROM the GREAT BEAST HIMSELF!

=AHEM= VELL, IF I MUST... FIRST VE'LL DISCUSS DER PART OF DE PSYCHE I CALL DER COLLECTIVE UNCONSCIOUS, UND DER ARCH TYPES VITHIN--DER MYTHOLOGICAL IMAGES DOT CONTAIN A PAR OF HUMAN PSYCHOLOGY UND FATE. DEN VE'LL DISCUSS PERSONALITY TYPES, SYNCHRONICITY, AUTOMATIC WRITING, ALCHEMY UND ASTROLOGY, UND HOW DIS ALL TIES INTO MY DREAMS UF DEAD PEOPLE, DWARVES, MAIDENS UND DRAGONS--

EXTRA **DAILY NEWS** FINAL

NEW YORK'S PICTURE NEWSPAPER

VOL 17. NO 103 — 72 PAGES — NEW YORK, THURSDAY, MAY 2, 1947 — 7 CENTS 1-

JUNG JAILED AFTER 22 DIE IN RIOT

137 COLLECTIVELY KNOCKED UNCONSCIOUS

STORY PG 3

MILLIONS MORE UPSET AND CONFUSED BY CRACKPOT THEORIES

SWISS PSYCHOLOGISTS VOW TO FREE ASSOCIATE

D.A. SAYS, "NIX". DOCS SAY, "MERCY." D.A. THEN SAYS, "JUSTICE." DOCS THEN SAY, "COMPASSION."

EXCLUSIVE PHOTO - JUNG ENCOUNTERS PRISON ARCHETYPES IN RIKER'S

— MORE PHOTOS PAGES 36, 37

COMING SOON-- SON OF JUNG!!!

...WHAT DOES IT LOOK LIKE I'M DOING?
evan 95
OH CRAP!
STOP YELLING!
BUT "COPS" IS ON!
SHIT!
DAMN!
WOULD YOU RELAX?
LOST BOY
HI!
GOOD DAY
FAMOUS FUCK-HEADS of FILM LAND
CAPT. LOW I.Q.
CITIZEN O-TRON
666
17 yr. old confused and sad girl on Ricki Lake Show 3/25/94
YOUR BAND HERE
Green slime.
DESTROY ALL RETAILERS!
BOOM!
COMICS
ROCKET FROM THE CRYPT
HOW TO DRAW MILK & CHEESE
EARTHLING! I HAVE TO PEE!
See jungle see jungle go join your gang, yeah-
HEY!
I've been practicing my free association!
JUST OUT!
Ri-
Very sleepy. Just let me sleep...
BUT BAY-BEH! I'M YO SKELLY MAN!
THIS IS NEW
Hitler. Always funny.
Danke!
A&E
SO?
BOOM!
JINX
PIXEL
EVAN
SARAH
and
ACTION TIM
HUEVOS RANCHEROS
IT'S A NO-REPEAT TUESDAY
YES!
Here I go!
Call Stephen-inks?
MR POTATO TURD © TM BIG FUCK
Comic Culture cover-March 5th or 15th? call
THINK VINNIE!! the C-INK! DON'T THINK!
21ST CENT
M&C promo card - a.s.a.p.
? 45-no border
cheaper 50-with
2½ by 3½ live area
Tues/Wed?
- need catalogues!!!
monopoly house
postage stamp
EAT MORE LEKVAR! OK!
EVIL
please God-more Star Wars
FEB-14th-DAY FUCK HALLMARK
A
GLOSS
HAPPY BRATWURST YES!!!
Call Thakston- where the fuck is my page?
Send Jeff H-S. Ghost tape
-call MOM-
Prince Namor approves?
A.P.E. II - 13th?
FUCK HIM!

Stutterers Anonymous by "Stuar

fin?

Please stand by
we are experiencing
technical difficulties

CALIFORNIA WHINE COUNTRY
:snif: no waves today, dude!
:sob: my band broke up!
:sigh: my cult broke up!
my t.v. series got bad reviews!
this gun never works!
No producers will screw me for a role!

the BUM and his ASSISTANT BUM
'ey... get me that nickel, willya? I'm busy over here...
You got it, J.B.!
CAMEL

ONFUSE the MAN WHO is MAD AT YOU!
YOU SON OF A BITCH!
Oh, so you've met my mother.
uh... HAH?

RANDOM THOUGHT #1
When Edison came up with the idea for the light bulb... did he see one above his head when the notion hit him? See what I'm getting at?
OR perhaps-
THINGS TO DO 1) invent 2) fuck Tesla over patent

RESTAURANT JOKE!
WELCOME TO - FRIENDLY'S
THANKS! COME AGAIN REAL SOON!
HAVE A NICE DAY
can I have--
FUCK YOU.
WELCOME TO FRIENDLY'S It's A PLEASURE SERVING YOU
FRIENDLY'S

T IS TO LAFF DEPT...
I told you- NO! Now leave me ALONE!
BAR
ERE IS NO JOY IN MUDVILLE...
CHAEL CASEY HAS STRUCK OUT.

TONIGHT'S FORECAST...
DOUBT
HATE
DARK
BLEAKNESS
COLD
UNCERTAINTY
ANXIETY
FEAR
VIOLENCE
CHILLS
TRAUMA
PRESSURE
NOISE
PANIC
DESPAIR
STAY HOME... STAY HOME... STA

MADISON AVE. FUCK-UP

We switched Betty Arnold's husband with a scarecrow to prove a point! This was twelve years ago and frankly, we forgot why we did it in the first place.

RODUCT DISPLACEMENT
up yours, sshole!
jerk.
LIQUID CLEANSER WITH ABRASIVE
LIQUID CLEANSER WITH MILD ABRASIVE

All right, okay- that's enough of that! Let's see... what's this written here... "MEN- ask yourselves- what would you rather come home to find-- a man beating your wife or making love to her?" Whaat? Where'd I come up with that? I don't think people are gonna get what that means... it's gonna sound bad... oh, forget it...

Um, before we get to this next strip, here's an idea I've been working on. You know when there's some bullshit sports fan riot after some stupid championship game that their dumb local team's won?

WE'RE #1!
our piss-poor lives have been given meaning!
WE'RE #1 even tho' we didn't do anything!
Dallas is the best! Let's trash it!

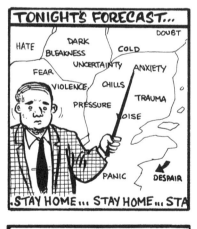

Here's what I think should be done- While these clueless neanderthals revel over their tribal bullshit-- Helicopters should dump dyes- like those the banks use to mark stolen money- all over the stupid fucking mob of monkey fucks--
COWBOYS

Then, days later, the police can still identify the morons because they're still marked by the "ASSHOLE PAINT©" and lock their pathetic asses up for, oh, for fucking ever...
Asshole- Asshole-
C'mon asshole.
Asshole -Asshole

It's just an idea of mine.
Anyway, I'm gonna jump up and down on the bed while you read the next strip. See you soon!
ACTION GIRL

The Junkies

by Dorkin, Boyce & Har

Here we come-- -pissin' on the streeet-- we get the funniest looks from-- -everyone we meeeet--
SID LIVES

Hey Hey-we're the Junkies an' people say we fuck up the town- -but we're too busy scoring- -to... to... uh-um... hm-hmm...

we're just trying to be... uh er, something... -come and watch us sit-- --uh, er, around-- -we're the young generatio ...and we've got... uh... nothin to... ummm... saaaaay...
hey hey... we're the junkies...
huh?
hey... hey...
hey, hey, we're t ...what are we?
hey what
huh..?
huh...
uhh...

There was more to that strip, but I got bored. I think drug humor is pretty fucking dull, anyway. I don't know why, but for me drunks are funny and addicts just-
Meanwhile, in the kitchen of G. Gordon Liddy-
OW! FUCK! AHHH! I BURNT MY FINGER! OWIE!
S.M.C.

What the fuck was that? I was still talking back there! Shit! This is what happens when you work without an edi-
THERE'S A LADY WHO'S SURE-- -ALL THAT GLITTERS IS GOLD-
HEY- what's that noise? Who doused the lights?
INSTANT PIANO #4 THE END!

OH, SHIT! IT'S LASER ZEPPELIN! NOT AGAIN!
AND SHE'S BUY-YI-YING A STAIRW TO HEAV

THIS IS THE WAY IT IS...,
I'M WALKING DOWN
NG FLIGHTS OF STAIRS...
IN TOTAL DARKNESS...

IN EACH OF MY HANDS
I'M HOLDING A HEAVY GLASS,
BOTH OF WHICH ARE FILLED
WITH SOME KIND OF LIQUID...

I HAVE TO BE VERY CAREFUL,
I'M AFRAID I'LL DROP A GLASS.
I DON'T WANT TO SPILL ANY
OF THE LIQUID...

CAN'T SEE A THING
D I'M DEATHLY AFRAID
LOSING MY BALANCE...

IF I DO LOSE MY BALANCE,
I'LL FALL, BECAUSE MY
HANDS ARE FULL...

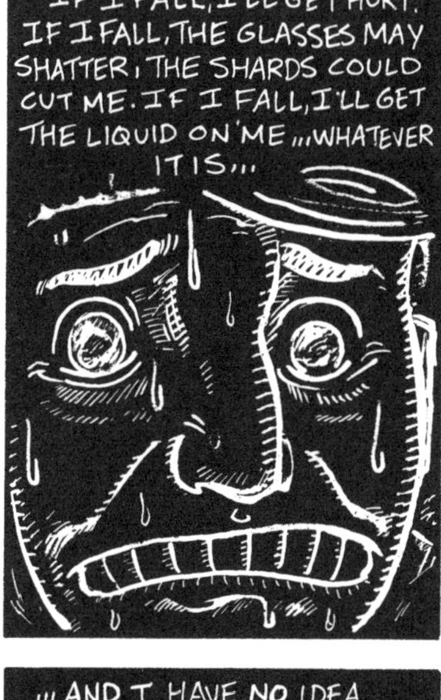

IF I FALL, I'LL GET HURT.
IF I FALL, THE GLASSES MAY
SHATTER, THE SHARDS COULD
CUT ME. IF I FALL, I'LL GET
THE LIQUID ON ME... WHATEVER
IT IS...

F I FALL I
MIGHT NEVER
STOP FALLING...

THIS IS ALL I CAN THINK
ABOUT WITH EACH AND EVERY
CAUTIOUS STEP. WHAT MAKES
IT WORSE IS - I DON'T KNOW
HOW MUCH FARTHER DOWN
I HAVE LEFT TO GO...

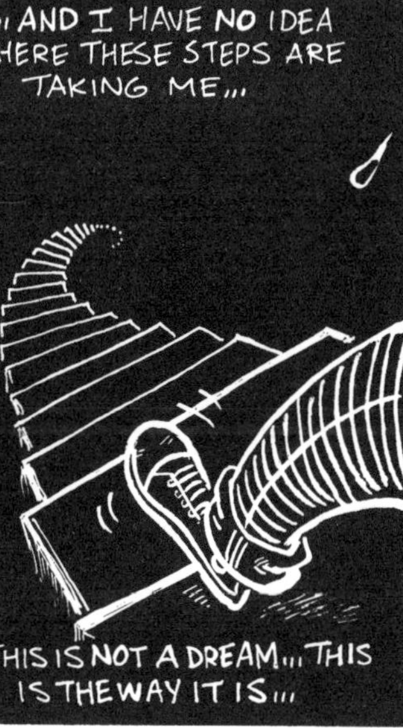

...AND I HAVE NO IDEA
WHERE THESE STEPS ARE
TAKING ME...
THIS IS NOT A DREAM... THIS
IS THE WAY IT IS...

--uh, sorry 'bout that. That slipped in. Actually, that page was supposed to have a **really good** leper gag, Really funny, lotsa **yocks. HA-HA.**

I guess I'm **slipping** up a bit. Um, I've been under a lot of pressure lately. Bad hours, bad sleep. A neck injury's causing me to see a doctor twice a week, and I'm uninsured, etc., etc., blah blah, middle class whine. There's a lot on my mind lately...

The whole comic industry is a bi fucking **wreck** these days and I can't seem to stop worrying about it. I'm **sick of worrying** abou what **some company** does, or what distributor does, or what retailer don't do, or how everyone seems want the same old fucking cra over and over and over and OVE

Anyway, let's not get into that... I only have so many pages here and talking about comics already takes up too much of my life... Fucking comics. I swear... I just wish things wouldn't bother me so much so I could just relax for a single fucking second some day.

For some reason, I've **been having** this irrational fear of getting bad **PAPER CUTS** across my fingers lately. I think about it a LOT...

This always leads me to thinking of having razor blades slicing m open. I don't know why I thin about this so often- I'm alway pulling my sleeves up or graspin my wrists as if to ward off a phantom slashing. It's **bizarre**.

I'm literally cringing now as I write this- ah, fuck, why am I even getting into this- this wasn't in my layouts! Shit! Now I'm thinking about slashed wrists! **MY** slashed wrists! And for some screwy reason, thinking about **bleeding** makes me start thinking about **FLYING!**

I am absolutely traumatized by **FLYING**- even though I've flown fairly often and continue to get on planes. I **never** used to have this problem and **now** it's gotten to the point where I have fucking **panic attacks** over flying---

I know I have to fly to the we Coast later this year and I'm alre obsessing about it. I have terrib nightmares about flying... the fai takeoff... the rush of wind... the sound of impact--

Sometimes when I drive on the Jersey turnpike or the Belt Parkway I'll stare up at planes in the sky and start to panic. I'll probably die in a car crash this way- forget a fucking plane wreck.

Oh, man... I've totally lost track here- I don't even know what the point was to this. If it was some cathartic therapy thing it sure as hell isn't working. Fuck. **FUCK!!** I better quit this before the whole 'death business' takes over the rest of the goddam strip...

I hope you guys aren't pissed of I know, I wasted a page or tw that could've been jokes, or so Milk and Cheese strip or somethin Sorry, sorry. At least the last panel was sort of funny, with Death guy scaring me and all...

of course, I'm also terrified of cancer and AIDS and nuclear war and fire and having a stroke or being shot or...or...

Reader's Survey #15
Where do you read comics?

- In bed.
- At work.
- On the can.
- In the comics shop so I don't have to buy them.
- In the newspapers. That Cathy really cracks me up.
- On the bus to incur public ridicule.
- ❒ I don't read comics. Nothing wrong with me, pal, fuck you!
- ❒ In the crawlspace, here where I keep my victims.
- ❒ In my own private fantasy world far from all who do not understand me.

lease send answers to: Survey, c/o this comic. Trained chimps are on hand to open your responses and throw them away!!

There are so many things I could have said in this panel and all I did was fucking waste it. Another blown opportunity. I could've changed the world...

zzZZ

Okay, a note about the next quick bit. It's a pun, or something, on a gospel musical, so if you don't know the play, no big deal. It's nothing great, but it's been in my files for years and I just wanted to do it, okay? So sue me.

YOUR ARMS ARE TOO SHORT TO BOX WITH GOD

DING!

. Maybe I should've left that in my files. Oh, well. I'm not together here, am I? In t, this is my third attempt at s panel. I didn't like what I originally, so I pasted a new el down, but that sucked, so you get this one. Don't worry, n all the comics distributors refuse to carry small press ks and we'll all just disappear you won't be bothered with likes of me anymore. But, ore I go, we still have this p, so I better make with ne jokes...

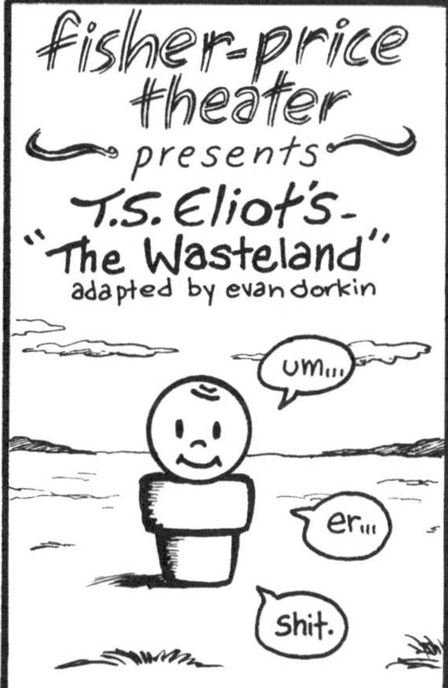
fisher-price theater
presents
T.S. Eliot's "The Wasteland"
adapted by evan dorkin
um...
er...
Shit.

WAIT! STOP!! I'M SORRY, I CAN'T GO THROUGH WITH THIS STRIP! I DON'T KNOW A FUCKING THING ABOUT the WASTELAND! I read it in college and I couldn't understand a single goddam word of it! I'm sorry, I really am... I don't know what I was trying to pull there. Look, I'll try to do a real strip, honest I will!!

Do I still get paid?
TURN THE PAGE AND PRAY

This was a city. A thriving. bustling metropolis. Now it's a charred cinder... a graveyard.

My name is Steve Marsten... I'm a reporter... at least I was... until yesterday -- -- the day HE came.
It all started two days ago...

...with the strange reports of scor
of fish washing ashore ... along
with loaves of bread. Scientist
were baffled - no cargo ships ha
been reported damaged. Even mo
disturbing were two new discoveri
WONDER

The fish and loaves were high
radioactive, and the offshore wate
were found to be chemically
consistent with cheap table win
But this was only the beginnin

Because the next day--**HE AROSE!**

CHRISTZILLA

He's alive!

KING OF THE MESSIAHS

EAT LEKVAR

KOOL

CIVILIZATION CRUMBLES - as his death stigmata rays blast a city of 10 million from the face of the earth

evan dorkin 2·95

He first appeared in the financial district... estroying everything in his wake. Soon he cut devastating, bloody path throughout the entire ity, attacking millions. **Why?** What did he **want?**

No one could begin to comprehend these swiftly unfolding events-- while some looked to the heavens, scientists were theorizing that the gargantuan savior had been reborn from experimental atomic testing...

lothing could stop him! Tanks- planes- infantry-- ven high-tension electrical wires- Christzilla as impervious to the war machines of man!

The creature's very being brought the government and military into conflict as to how to deal with it. Some refused to fight, while others pressed for the attack...

BUT SIR-WHAT ABOUT THE BOMB?
You mean, dropping the atomic bomb on Christzilla?!?
IT COULD WORK!
ARE YOU INSANE, MAN? MY MOTHER WOULD NEVER SPEAK TO ME AGAIN!!

Then- as suddenly and mysteriously as he had
ppeared-- the massive form of Christzilla
urned away from the city...
and stepped out
onto the ocean...
leaving the
survivors in
bewilderment.
CHRISTZILLAA!! COME BAACK!!
?!

SO WHAT REALLY HAPPENED HERE?
WAS IT THE SECOND COMING?!
WAS IT SCIENCE GONE AWRY?!?
BUT-SCIENTIFICALLY SPEAKING-IT'S IMPOSSIBLE FOR CHRIST TO BE SO HUGE! HIS LEGS COULDN'T SUPPORT HIS WEIGHT!
THAT'S BECAUSE IT'S A MIRACLE, YOU DOLT!
MIRACLE? THAT THING STEPPED ON MY WIFE!
I'M CONFUSED! WHAT HAPPENS NOW?!
COMING SOON!!!
KING KONG
VS.
CHRISTZILLA!

Panel missing.

What? Oh, wow, sorry-my fault. I wasn't paying attention... I thought there was another page to the last strip. I'm really not too on top of my game here. Oh well, I'll see it when it prints. Can't worry about it now I guess. I have enough to think about. Something bad kind of happened this week... anyway, I really don't feel like discussing it here. I'm not even going to fix that lettering fuck up up there. I'm just too pissed off to care...

GOD, what I wouldn't give for an army of zombies under my total command...

Actually, to be honest, and I have given this a lot of thought, what I'd really like to be is the fabled KING of the CHIMPS and DWARVES!

FAIR PLAY

We'd have our own place somewhere where we'd work together as a society and no one would bother us. We'd still have cable and Coca-cola and all, don't get me wrong, it's just we'd help each other out and have a lot of fun and all. Like a children's book, you know?

HUZZAH!
AND THEY WERE ALL SO FUCKING HAPPY IT MADE THEM PUKE.
THE END.

I guess the Zombie Army cou
lurk around the edges of the woods in case anyone tried to fuck with us...

Are you talking abo that monk world of yo again
NO! And besides, it's chimps! An dwarves, to And you and cats and any we like wh wants to vis

God, you're so insane...
Well, if I am, all the worse for you, then!
Why don't you tell them about that ridiculous t.v. thing you've been on about while you're at it!?
All right, I will! Nyah!
NO SLOGAN

Sometimes, when I watch old television shows... hearing the audience laughing depresses the hell out of me...

ohhhh, Rob!

I wonder to myself--who were those people? Where are they now? Do they ever watch for that sho to hear the sounds of when the were young and happy? Would they need to be reminded tha there once was such a time?

Then I think, schmuck--get a gri It's the fucking Dick Van Dyke Sho

But I can't stop feeling bummed out by those anonymous, faceless old audiences. Most of the people are probably dead now, but they're still yuckin' it up on the t.v, ha-ha, big joke, big fuckin' joke, cause you're all dead or dying and it's some big 'joke, one big disappointment after another and then it's over and they're still laughing and it wasn't so funny in the first place, was it?

Ah, fuck this-I don't even know what I'm talking about-don't listen to me. I meant to close with a joke and now I'm out of room. Maybe that's the joke, and I just don't get it. So sue me. I'm outta here... Thanks for being here. I mean it.

Good night, Mrs. Calabash...
...wherever you are.

Three... two... one... stop. STOP.

BUT THAT WAS OUR OR FIVE YEARS AGO--
WHAT'S BECOME OF THE WHINY LITTLE CRETIN NOW?
CAN HE FLY? IS HE STILL OBSESSED WITH DYING?
HAS THE COMIC INDUSTRY DIED?
HAS THAT POOR GIRL WISED UP AND LEFT HIM?
YEAH, AN' JUST WHAT WAS THAT DWARF AN' CHIMP JAZZ..?
COME NOW, CLUE US IN LOVE-- YOU DO KNOW EVERYTHING!
AH, INDEED I DO.
"AND YES, I DO HAVE THE LATEST SCUTTLEBUTT ON OUR NEUROTIC LITTLE CARTOONIST FRIEND. FIRST OF ALL, HIS LONG-SUFFERING GIRLFRIEND IS STILL SUFFERING."
ECONDLY, THE COMICS DUSTRY HAS NOT DIED. OT YET, AT LEAST."
THE COMIC INDUSTRY 1933-???
NOW?
NOT YET.
"CRAWLS ALONG-- GUTSHOT AND OUGHING UP FOUR-COLOR BLOOD S IT SWALLOWS ITS OWN TAIL."
BUT DESPITE THAT, OUR BOY'S CAREER HAS ACTUALLY FLOURISHED ...BELIEVE IT OR NOT. HE'S WON SEVERAL AWARDS FOR HIS QUESTIONABLE WORK-- AND HE'S BEEN WRITING STEADILY FOR T.V. ANIMATION FOR THE PAST SEVERAL YEARS--
OH...SO HE'S GOTTEN HIS ACT TOGETHER. HOW ...UNINTERESTING.
I WAS KIND OF HOPING HE KILLED HIMSELF.
ME TOO!
AH, REJOICE, DEAR HEARTS! FOR OUR BOY HASN'T BEEN ABLE TO ACTUALLY ENJOY HIS PIDDLING LITTLE SUCCESS.
YOU SEE, HE BEGAN TO FEEL PRESSURED FROM THE ATTENTION HIS WORK WAS RECEIVING, AND THIS ADDED TO HIS ALREADY FESTERING ANXIETIES, WHICH IN TURN EXACERBATED HIS DEEPENING DEPRESSION--
--AND ULTIMATELY LED TO A FULL-BLOWN NERVOUS BREAK-DOWN IN AUGUST OF 1996, DAYS BEFORE A FLIGHT TO A COMIC BOOK CONVENTION.
YOU MIGHT BE UNHAPPY TO HEAR THAT SINCE THEN, THERAPY AND MEDICATION HAVE ALLOWED HIM TO FLY AGAIN.
HE HAS ALSO BEGUN TO DRAW AGAIN, AFTER AN EIGHT MONTH DRY SPELL.
BUT REST ASSURED-- HE IS STILL QUITE MISERABLE.
AH, SO WHAT?! ANOTHER NEUROTIC JEW IN THE ENTERTAINMENT INDUSTRY, WHOOP-DE-DOO!
MADELINE, PLEASE! OUR HOST IS A MEMBER OF THE TRIBE!
HE'S AFRICAN?
ALL I WANT TO KNOW IS WHAT'S THE DEAL WITH THE DWARVES AND CHIMPS?
AND THE ZOMBIES. LET US NOT FORGET THE LEGIONS OF THE UNDEAD.
I BET HE WAS ABUSED AS A KID. I MEAN, MONKEYS AND MIDGETS? IT'S PRETTY PERVERTED IF YOU ASK ME--
TELL US, DEVIL PUPPET-- JUST HOW DO YOU KNOW ALL OF THESE THINGS?
AH, YES... THE ETERNAL QUESTION ...
I WAS ASKED THAT ONCE WHILE DINING WITH JOHN CAGE AND THE ARCHITECT PHILIP JOHNSON--
A-HA! THERE YOU ARE!!
OH DEAR. THE MAL-ADJUSTED SPOIL-SPORT'S HERE.
OH-NO!
PLEASE DON'T TAKE HIM FROM US!
WHAT ABOUT OUR STOCK TIPS?
HE HASN'T TOLD US HEMINGWAY'S LAST WORDS YET!
THAT'S HIM? HE'S REALLY UGLY IN PERSON!

GOD AM I SORRY I EVER STARTED DRAWING YOU! ALL YOU DO IS CAUSE ME GRIEF!
THIS RELATIONSHIP GETS MORE PARASITIC AND LESS SYMBIOTIC EVERY DAMNED DAY!

I DON'T KNOW WHY YOU'RE SO UPSET--
--IT'S NOT LIKE I TOLD ANY TRULY EMBARRASSING ANECDOTES ABOUT YOU... LIKE THE PHONE SEX STORY--
HEH HEH-OKAY, LET'S NOT--

OR THAT TIME YOU TRIED TO COMMIT SUICIDE BY WALK-ING INTO THE OCEAN--
-- BUT TURNED BACK WHEN YOU REALIZE YOUR WALLET WAS GETTING WET?
Yeah, WELL-
AND DEPRESS

THANK GOD MY JEWBOY MONEYLUST SAVED ME--
OR THAT TIME YOU PICKED UP THE GIRL IN THE "ROGUE" COS-TUME AT THE SAN DIEGO COMIC CONVE
NOW WAITAMINNIT! SHE WASN'T WEAR-ING A GODDAM COSTUME WHEN I HIT ON HER AND YOU KNOW IT!
WELL, THEN, WHAT ABOUT--

LISTEN YOU LITTLE LEGLESS SATANIC FUCK! YOU CAN SHUT THE HELL UP NOW!!
AHEM... ...YOU KNOW HOW MUCH I DETEST IT WHEN YOU USE SUCH LANGUAGE.
OH, PARDONNEZ-MOI!

YOU WANT WITTY AND URBANE BANTER, GO DIG UP NOEL COWARD AND CHANNEL YOUR PUPPETY ASS OFF!
I'LL ASK YOU TO LEAVE MY FRIEN OUT OF THIS, IF YOU PLEASE.
I'D LIKE TO LEAVE YOU SOMEWHERE YOU GOSSIPY PLASTIC SHITBA

I'LL HAVE YOU KNOW THAT YOUR CONSTANT USE OF VULGARITY IS A SURE SIGN OF AN IMMATURE, UNDEVELOPED PERSONALITY.
Y'KNOW, I'M SURE I COULD DEVASTATE YOU WITH SOME OH-SO-CUTTING BON MOT--
--BUT WHY BOTHER WHEN "FUCK YOU, PUPPET" GETS RIGHT TO THE POINT?

YOU MIS-PRONOUNCED "BON MOT."
FUCK YOU, PUPPET.

SWEETIE! I'M HOME!
SORRY I'M LATE--
--I HAD TO STOP THE DEVIL PUPPET AGAIN.

WHAT WAS HE UP TO THIS TIME?
OH, RUNNING UP BAR TABS, STEALING MEMORIES, RE-VEALING MY INNER-MOST SECRETS TO PEOPLE. Y'KNOW, THE USUAL.
BOO!
WELL THAT SUCKS.
ANYWAY, HOW WAS THERAPY?

UHHH...
OKAY, I GUESS

EVERY DAY SARAH ASKS ME, "WHAT'S WRONG?"
WIRED WORLD

WHAT'S WRONG IS THAT EVERY DAY SARAH HAS TO ASK ME, "WHAT'S WRONG?" BECAUSE THERE'S ALWAYS SOMETHING WRONG. BECAUSE I'M ALWAYS MISERABLE... I'M CONSTANTLY ANXIOUS OR WORRIED OR FRUSTRATED OR ANGRY OR... WORSE.
I SHOULD BE HAPPY... I HAVE A GOOD LIFE, BETTER THAN I EVER DREAMED OF HAVING... I DON'T KNOW WHAT IT IS.
I'M JUST NOT HAPPY.

I'VE NEVER BEEN A HAPPY PERSON. I WAS A MISERABLE KID, SCARED AND CONFUSED BY EVERYTHING... AND IT'S JUST GOTTEN WORSE AS I'VE GOTTEN OLDER... NOW MY FEARS AND ANXIETIES ARE OUT OF CONTROL AND I'M HAVING THESE PANIC ATTACKS...
AND I'M JUST SO FUCKING SICK OF FEELING LIKE SHIT ALL THE TIME.
I'M JUST SO TIRED... TIRED OF EVERYTHING. I MEAN--
WIRED WORLD

THE ONLY THING I LOOK FORWARD TO ANYMORE IS GOING TO SLEEP... WHEN I CAN SLEEP, THAT IS.
WANT TO HEAR SOMETHING FUNNY? YOU KNOW THAT SAYING--
--"A DREAM IS A WISH YOUR HEART MAKES?"
LAST NIGHT I DREAMT I DIED.

GHOST
THESAURUS
TCH. SHIT.

OH MY GOD!! SOMEONE CALL THE HOSPITAL!
THERE'S BEEN A FREAK ACCIDENT!

HMMM...
QUIET. IT'S FINE.

I THINK IT'S FUNNY!
YOU WOULD.
AHEM! DO YOU MIND? I'M TRYING TO WORK HERE!
GO RIGHT AHEAD! WE'RE JUST WATCHING--IT'S BEEN A WHILE! AND DON'T YOU WORRY--
--YOU WON'T EVEN KNOW WE'RE HERE! PROMISE!

INSTEAD OF BOLSTERING MY LO SELF-ESTEEM AND CONFIDEN --THE AWARDS AND ATTENTION MADE ME FEEL PRESSURED I BEGAN TO SECOND-GUES EVERYTHING I DID--EVERY DRAWING... EVERY IDEA... AN EVERY LINE OF DIALOGUE.
BEHOLD! WE ARE MILK AND CHEESE!
BEHOLD! WE'RE MILK AND CHEESE!
BEHO WE AR THE DA DUO
OH HO! WE'RE MILK AND CHEESE!
HUZZAH! WE'RE MILK AND CHEESE!

WAS TERRIFIED OF A BACK-
LASH AGAINST MY WORK. I
ELT I HAD TO CONSISTENTLY
OP MYSELF OR FACE FAILURE
ND RIDICULE. NOBODY PUT
HIS CRIPPLING PRESSURE ON
E--I HEAD-FUCKED MYSELF.

I HATED HIS STUFF BEFORE IT WAS COOL TO HATE HIS STUFF!
$ELL OUT!
SAME OLD SHIT!
UN-FUNNY!
LOATHE MAIL

OSTLY IMAGINED REACTIONS FROM
MOSTLY IMAGINARY READERS...)

EVENTUALLY I BECAME UNABLE TO COMMIT ANYTHING TO PAPER. I HAD ZERO CONFIDENCE AND I NO LONGER TRUSTED MY INSTINCTS AND I SECOND AND THIRD AND FIFTEENTH-GUESSED MYSELF INTO A CREATIVE COMA.

YOU SUCK!
YOU CAN'T DO ANY-THING RIGHT!
YOU LACK VISION!
YOU'RE NOT FUNNY!
PAPER WORK
UN-ANSWERED MAIL

(ACTUAL REACTIONS FROM ACTUAL BRAIN)

LOOK--I KNOW MY PROBLEMS GO FAR BEYOND MY WORK SITUATION--BUT IT TIES INTO EVERYTHING ELSE. IT'S LIKE... DEEP DOWN I'M JUST AFRAID PEOPLE WILL CONFIRM THE THINGS THAT I'VE ALWAYS BELIEVED ABOUT MYSELF...

...THAT I'M A NO-TALENT.
A BIG-MOUTHED PHONY.
A LUCKY FRAUD.

BUT WHAT IF I AM A FRAUD? I MEAN... WHAT CAN YOU DO WHEN THE BEST YOU CAN DO MIGHT BE WORTHLESS? WE CAN'T ALL BE AS SMART OR AS TALENTED AS WE WOULD LIKE TO BE, RIGHT?! WE CAN'T ALL BE BRILLIANT! ALL WE CAN DO IS WORK HARD AND DO OUR BEST-- AM I RIGHT?!

I'D SAY SO--

WELL THAT SUCKS!

UHH, CAN I ASK YOU SOMETHING? HAVE YOU CONSIDERED TAKING SOME ART CLASSES TO STRENGTHEN YOUR DRAWING SKILLS?

YEAH, I'VE THOUGHT OF THAT.
DORKIN, E - 6/10/98
-ATTENTION DEFICIT... ...DISORDER
-GENERAL ANXIETY DISORDER
-OBSESS/COMP-
-PASSIVE/AGGRESSIVE
-DIARRHEA OF THE

BUT I'VE ALSO THOUGHT ABOUT KILLING CARTOONISTS WHO ARE BETTER THAN ME AND EATING THEIR HEARTS SO I CAN GAIN THEIR ABILITIES.

HERNAND G.
STEPHENS J.
ELDER, W.
DESTEFAN S.
HERNANDEZ J.
ROOT BEER

ACTUALLY, I'LL TELL YOU WHAT I'VE THOUGHT ABOUT--QUITTING. THE DRAWING, THAT IS. I'M SURE IT WOULD MAKE SOME FOLKS HAPPY.

JOE'S COMICS
COMICS GULAG
WIZARD
NOTHING ABOUT EVAN DORKIN QUITTING
CBG
PETER DAVID SEES A MOVIE, EATS FOOD
THE GUY WHO DID "BILL AND TED'S" QUITS DRAWING. RETAILERS CHEER NO ONE ELSE NOTICES
HULK SMASHED!
I STINK
FUND STARTED TO GET HIM TO QUIT WRITING AS WELL
MAYBE EVEN ME.

EEZ LOUISE WHAT A ROCK OF SHIT! WHAT RE YOU TRYIN' TO DO KILL OFF SALES?
AT LEAST THE HEART EATING BIT WAS KINDA COOL!
OH, IT WAS PERFECTLY SERVICEABLE AS FAR AS CANNIBALISM JOKES GO. HOWEVER...
FOR THE VERY LAST
CHALAND
MYLANTA
CHERRY CREME

MUST EVERYTHING BE A REFERENCE TO COMICS? I MEAN, REALLY NOW MY BOY, EXPAND YOUR HORIZONS--
I KNOW, I KNOW! WHAT CAN I TELL YOU-- I'M OBSESSED WITH COMIC BOOKS!
BELIEVE YOU ME, I'M TRYING TO WEAN MYSELF OFF THE SUB-JECT--BUT IT'S A HARD TEAT TO ABANDON, DRIED OUT AND FLACCID AS IT MAY BE--

H, STOP APOLOGIZING! COMICS ARE A SERIOUS EDIUM WORTHY OF EXAM-ATION AND ALL THAT MICS JOURNAL BULLSHIT HEN WHAT'S WRONG WITH HE MAN DISCUSSING 'EM?
HA! LISTEN TO YOURSELF! WHO'S THE APOLOGIST NOW, MY FRIEND?
WHO? HAH?

ANYHOO... WHAT HE'S DOING ISN'T EXAMINING COMICS AS A MEDIUM. HE'S SIMPLY BITCHING AND MOANING, OR EMPLOYING OBSCURE REFERENCES FOR CHEAP GAGS ONLY COMIC FANS WILL GET--

SO?
AHEM- CAN WE TALK ABOUT SOMETHING OTHER THAN COMICS?
WHAT'S THE POINT? HE'LL STILL BE THINK-ING ABOUT COMICS--

MARVEL COMICS RECESSION FUNNIES:

HYDRA BUDGET:

"I DON'T KNOW WHAT TO DO--EVERYTIME WE FIRE A GUY, TWO MORE TAKE HIS PLACE!"

SEE?! WHAT DID I TELL YOU? PATHETIC!
I DIDN'T EVEN GET IT.
IT'S A MARVEL REFERENCE. DON'T WORRY ABOUT IT.
:SIGH: COMICS. IT ALWAYS COMES BACK TO COMICS...
TELL ME A LITTLE ABOUT YOUR FATHER.
WELL... THERE ISN'T A LOT TO SAY.
WHICH SAYS A LOT, I GUESS.

INSTEAD OF DOING THINGS WITH US OR TALKING TO US HE'D BUY US THINGS, EVERY SUNDAY HE'D TAKE US TO THE TE-AMO ON KING'S HIGHWAY AND LET US BUY ALL THE COMICS WE WANTED.
MARVELS FOR ME.
ARCHIES AND HARVEYS FOR MY SISTER.

WELL... THAT'S AN INTERESTING CONNECTION BETWEEN YOUR FATHE AND YOUR WORK, WOULDN'T YOU SAY
WH-WHAT DO YOU MEAN?
THOSE COMIC BOOKS--THE ONES HE BOUGHT YOU EVERY SUNDAY.
HAVE YOU EVER THOUGHT OF THAT?

--YOU SEE, HYDRA WAS THIS EVIL ORGANIZATION--
HEY!
WHAT ARE YOU DOING WEARING THE DEVIL PUPPET?!?

I LIKE HIM. HE'S KOOKY.
AW, RELAX! BESIDES, I ALWAYS WEAR THE DEVIL PUPPET!

"KOOKY?" DID YOU JUST USE THE WORD "KOOKY" IN MY COMIC?!
WHAT DO YOU MEAN YOU ALWAYS WEAR THE DEVIL PUPPET?!?

I WEAR HIM WHEN YOU'RE ASLEEP.
WHAT?! WHEN I' ASLEEP?!
WE ALL WEAR PUPPETS WHEN YOU'RE ASLEEP!
YES... IT GIVES US SOMETHING TO DO AND HELPS US MAKE SURE THAT YOU HAVE NIGHTMARES

SEE? I WEAR THE JESUS PUPPET!
Hello.
AND I WEAR THE GOD PUPPET!
HOWDY HOWDY! I AM GOD. LOVE ME OR I WILL FLOOD THE WORLD!

AND BEFORE YOU GET ALL NUTTY ABOUT IT, LET ME ASSURE YOU THERE'S NOTHING SYMBOLIC IN THIS--
Yeah, WE JUST REALLY LIKE THE PUPPETS!
GRRR
PTHH!
THIS IS RIDICULOU I'LL HAVE YOU KNO THERE'S NO WAY IN HELL I'M DOING STRIPS WITH--WITH THOSE THING
AND WHAT'S MORE--"NUTTY" IS JUST AS BAD AS "KOOKY"!!

OKAY, OKAY!
JEEZ, LIGHTEN UP!
YEAH, DON'T GET ALL NUTTY!
AND WHY DON'T ANY OF YOU HAVE A MOSES PUPPET FOR CHRISSAKES?! I AM A JEW YOU KNOW!!

WHAT'S SO FUNNY?
Y-YOU'RE BARELY A JEW MY FRIEND!
YEAH! THE GUILT AND THE NOSE DOESN'T QUITE CUT IT!
HA HA HA HA HA HA HA HA HA HA HA HA
:SIGH:
ACTUALLY, HE'S NOT REALLY A JEW--HE'S JUST A BIT JEW-ISH!

NO.
I DON'T REALLY BELIEVE IN GOD. OR AN AFTERLIFE. I WISH I DID, BELIEVE YOU ME!
I'M SURE IT WOULD HELP ME DEAL WITH MY FEAR OF DEATH A LITTLE BETTER!

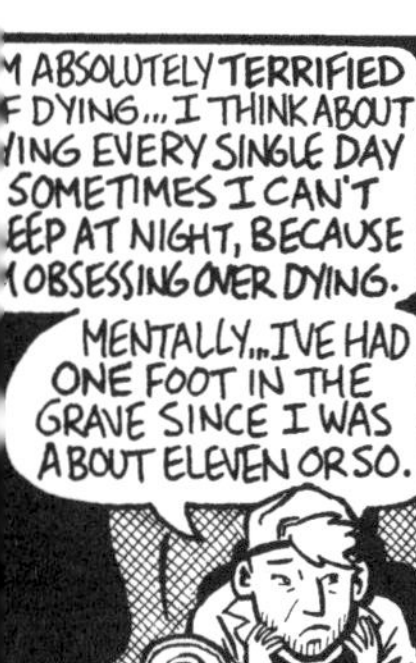
M ABSOLUTELY TERRIFIED
F DYING... I THINK ABOUT
ING EVERY SINGLE DAY
SOMETIMES I CAN'T
EEP AT NIGHT, BECAUSE
I OBSESSING OVER DYING.
MENTALLY... I'VE HAD ONE FOOT IN THE GRAVE SINCE I WAS ABOUT ELEVEN OR SO.
MILK
BREAD
ROUND BEEF (1/2 POUND)
T BLUE JUNK
THERINE LIKES
H TRAPS

WHEN I WAS LITTLE I'D WRAP MYSELF UP IN MY COVERS AT NIGHT, AND STAY COMPLETELY STILL TO TRY AND SEE WHAT IT WOULD BE LIKE TO BE DEAD AND BURIED.
BUT... IF I WAS REALLY DEAD... I WOULDN'T BE THINKING THIS.
-SOB-

OF COURSE, THE IDIOTIC THING IS THAT WHEN I WAS A TEENAGER I PULLED A LOT OF GOD-DAMNED STUPID SHIT THAT COULD HAVE GOTTEN ME KILLED!
EX.1 - HANGING OUT OF CARS GOING 80 MPH
EX.2 - TRYING TO JUMP FROM 4TH FLOOR WINDOW
SOBER
DRUNK
WASTED
SOBER
BELT PKWY E.
ASLEEP
3 LANE DRIFT AT 50 MPH
EX.3 - RUNNING UNDER A MOVING 18-WHEELER
EX.4 - DRIVING HOME DRUNK (OR WORSE)

SO WHY WOULD I PULL ALL THOSE STUNTS WHEN I'M SO AFRAID TO DIE?
MORONIC TEENAGE REBELLION? DEPRESSION? SELF-LOATHING? A DEATH WISH? MELODRAMATIC ATTENTION-GETTING BULLSHIT?
DON'T ANSWER THAT.
SO, WITH NO PROSPECTS
R FEMALE COMPANIONSHIP,
R LAD LEAVES THE FERRY
UB AND ARRIVES HOME
LITTLE AFTER FIVE A.M.--
--BLIND STINKING DRUNK.
HE IS ALSO, I MIGHT ADD, AN EIGHTEEN YEAR OLD VIRGIN.
DEPRESSED...
...LONELY--
1984
--AND EXTREMELY AHEM--HORNY.

SATURATED WITH BEER, VODKA AND THE PERFUME OF GIRLS WHO WOULDN'T MEET HIS EYES, LET ALONE HIM-- OUR DESPERATE, LIZARD-BRAINED LAD DECIDES TO CALL A SEX-PHONE LINE.
NOW, BACK THEN, THESE "SERVICES" WERE UNLIKE THE LIVE CHAT LINES ENJOYED BY TODAY'S ONANISTIC TYPES.
FOR A HIGHER-THAN NORMAL PRICED CALL YOU COULD LISTEN TO A SHORT, PRE-RECORDED TAPE LOOP OF ONE OR TWO WOMEN, TRYING NOT TO LAUGH WHILE AURALLY SIMULATING SEX ACTS WITH ONE ANOTHER --OR "WITH" CALLER #3,722 OF THE DAY.
1-555 JERK-OFF
ZERO

MAZINGLY ENOUGH, OUR INEBRIATED PRO-
GONIST IS ABLE TO RECALL FROM MEMORY
E OF THESE PHONE NUMBERS--EVEN THOUGH
AD SOBER HE CAN'T REMEMBER HIS SOCIAL
CURITY NUMBER OR HIS MOTHER'S BIRTHDAY.
E DIALS THE NUMBER--
OH, YEAH BABY, OOH, IT'S AS BIG AS A FLASH-LIGHT--
(YOU WISH)
PORK RINDS
(BUT YOU KNOW)
-- AND RECEIVES A STREAM OF FALSE DESIRE IN HIS EAR.

BUT ALAS! BEFORE OUR HERO CAN TAKE HIS MATTER INTO HIS OWN HANDS--
OH DADDY PUT IT IN OH YEAH YEAH!
--HE PROMPTLY PASSES OUT, SCANT SECONDS AFTER THE PHONE MESSAGE HAD BEGUN!

ALL THIS WAS FORGOTTEN WHEN HE AWAKENED THE NEXT AFTERNOON. HOW EVER, SEVERAL WEEKS LATER--
MOTHER-FUCKER!! YOU'RE TELLING THEM THE PHONE SEX STORY AREN'T YOU?!? AREN'T YOU?!?
YOU COCK-SUCKERS PULL THIS SHIT AND EXPECT ME TO GET ANY WORK DONE?!
HEY, RELAX! RELAX! IT'S NOT AS IF HE'S TELLING IT TO A BUNCH OF COMPLETE STRANGERS!

--SO A COUPLE OF WEEKS LATER HIS MOTHER GETS A PHONE BILL WITH A TWO HUNDRED DOLLAR CALL ON IT!!
HA HA HA
NO! YOU'RE KIDDING!
WAIT, THERE'S MORE!
"SO HIS MOTHER IS LIKE, "WHAT THE FUCK IS THIS?" SHE DOESN'T RECOGNIZE THE PHONE NUMBER, SO SHE CALLS IT TO SEE WHAT IT IS--"
OH MY GOD! HOWARD*-YOU'RE NOT GOING TO BELIEVE THIS! HA HA HA!
OOH, YEAH BABY!
FUCK MY PUSSY!
(* MY STEP-FATHER - EV)
"CONFRONTED WITH THE BILL THE POOR SCHMUCK HAD TO OWN UP TO HIS DIRTY LITTLE PHONE CALL".
OH SHIT! YOU KNOW WHAT MUST HAVE HAPPENED?
WHEN I PASSED OUT I MUST HAVE LEFT THE PHONE OFF THE HOOK SO I GOT CHARGED FOR THE TEN HOURS I SLEPT!
OH GOD THIS IS SO FUCKING EMBARRASSING.
UH...MOM? COULD YOU PLEASE STOP LAUGHING NOW?
M IS FOR MASTURBATOR
"HIS MOTHER GOT THE PHONE COMPANY TO RE MOVE THE CHARGE, MAIN ON THE ARGUMENT THA NO ONE WOULD LISTE TO A TAPE MESSAGE FO TEN HOURS STRAIGHT
HOWARD SAID FOR $200 YOU COULD'VE GOTTEN YOURSELF A GOOD HOOKER!! HA HAHA--
HA HA. THANKS MOM. I GO DIE NOW.
HEY! LET GO YOU FUCKERS! I TOLD YOU, I'VE HAD ENOUGH OF THIS!
I'M GOING TO BED!
AHH, C'MON CHIEF! YOU BARELY WORKED TONIGHT--
AND I'M EXHAUSTED FROM YOU BASTARDS! ALL OF YOU!!
NOW, NOW, JUST RELAX. WE'LL BE QUIET AND LEAVE YOU ALONE SO YOU CAN GET BACK TO WORK, O.K?
WELL... OKAY.
IF YOU PROMISE...
WE DO!!
uh, LOOK, I'M SORRY--
--BUT DON'T YOU FEEL THIS STRIP IS ALREADY FAR TOO CLUTTERED WITHOUT--
K-SNAP!
THAT'S-- IT!
UH-OH.
NOT AGAIN!
WHO THE FUCK AM I KIDDING? FUCK THIS! FUCK THIS SHIT!
STOP!
YOU'LL MESS UP THE STRIP!
WHAT--THIS THING?! THIS PIECE OF SHIT?! FUCK THIS STRIP! IT SUCKS!!
YOU KNO THAT
DORK
RRRII
ALL YOU EVER DO IS TELL ME HOW EVERYTHIN I EVER DO IS SHIT

I CAN'T STAND IT ANY MORE! CAN'T YOU LEAVE ME ALONE?! CAN'T YOU FUCKING LET ME BREATHE?!
GODDAMN IT...
...CAN'T YOU JUST LET ME BREATHE?
ARE YOU DONE NOW?
GET UP, YOU FUCKING PUSSY.
JUST WHAT THE FUCK ARE YOU CRYING ABOUT?!
DON'T YOU UNDERSTAND THERE'S HONEST SUFFERING IN THE WORLD YOU SOFT PINK PATHETIC PILE OF SHIT!
MAN, IF YOU THOUGHT WE WERE HARD ON YOU BEFORE..
OKAY.. THAT'S ENOUGH!
ALL OF YOU.. GET OUT!
NOW!
UH OH-- THE SKIRT!
QUICKLY YOU FOOL! PUT ME DOWN BEFORE I'M DONE A SERIOUS PHYSICAL HARM!
PFFT! OH PLEASE!
SHE AIN'T GONNA USE THAT THING!
...
POP!
AAAAAAAA
THEY'LL BE BACK ...
SHHH... I KNOW.
I'M SORRY... I REALLY AM TRYING... BUT THEY KEEP COMING BACK.
BUT THEY'RE WEAKER EVERY DAY. YOU'LL SEE ...EVERYTHING IS GOING TO BE OKAY.
WHERE DID YOU GET A GUN FROM, ANYWAY?
I ALWAYS HAD IT.
JUST IN CASE I EVER HAD TO KILL YOU.
:SNIFF:
OH SHIT!
MY SOUP'S BURNING! WILL YOU BE OKAY..?
yeah ...
GIRLY-GIRL

IT WOULD SOLVE A FEW THINGS...
...AT LEAST I'D GET SOME SLEEP.

C'MON FUCKER
C'MON FUCKER
C'MON YOU FUCKER!

SHIT.
WHO AM I FUCKING KIDDING? I DON'T WANT TO DIE!
WHAT A JERK. FUCKING MR. MELODRAMA.

BESIDES... IF I KILLED MYSELF I'D MISS WRESTLING MONDAY
HEY!

THESE AREN'T BULLETS--THAT THING WAS LOADED WITH PEZ!
HOW... KOOKY.

K-KRUNCH!
PTTTHH!
UCCH! STALE!

AH, SHIT.
GODDAMNED SUN'S COMING UP. WISH I WAS MORE TIRED.

DEVIL PUPPET--WILL YOU TELL ME A STORY?
Hmm... ALL RIGHT. BUT ONLY IF YOU PROMISE TO GO TO BED AFTERWARDS.
I PROMISE!

LET'S SEE... HAVE I EVER TOLD YOU THE STORY OF THE BOY WHO GOT EVERYTHING HE EVER WANTED?
NO!
WHAT HAPPENED?

NOTHING, YOU IMBECILE! NOBODY GETS EVERYTHING THAT THEY WANT!
EEEK!
NOW GO TO BED!

AND FOR GOODNESS SAKE DO TRY TO CHEER UP A BIT. YOU'VE BECOME QUITE WEARYING LATELY
Yeah Yeah...
MYLANTA CHERRY FLAVORED

THIS DEVELOPED FEAR OF FLYING... MY NEED TO AVOID CONFLICT... TO AVOID MAKING DECISIONS IN MY LIFE... MY OUTBURSTS AND TANTRUMS...

IDAHO POTATOES

5 LBS

-- MY ANGER TOWARDS MYSELF AND MY FAMILY... MY CONSTANT NEED FOR ATTENTION AND REASSURANCE... MY TAKING OUT MY FRUSTRATIONS ON THOSE CLOSE TO ME...

... BEING UNABLE TO WRITE GAGS FOR TALKING DAIRY PRODUCTS IS REALLY THE **LEAST** OF MY PROBLEMS.

R MORE YEARS THAN I CARE TO DMIT I'VE BEEN AN EMOTIONAL R-WRECK, SO WRAPPED UP IN SELF AND MY PROBLEMS NO AWS OF LIFE COULD EVER FREE ME.

OK, FOLKS-- **STEP BACK**, NOTHING TO SEE **HERE**!

I'VE BARRELLED THROUGH LIFE FUCKED UP AND ANGRY-- NEVER CONFRONTING **WHY** I WAS FUCKED UP AND ANGRY UNTIL IT WAS TOO LATE -- UNTIL MY ANXIETIES WENT **APESHIT** ALL OVER ME AND I LOST THE ABILITY TO FUNCTION **DAY TO DAY**. THE FEAR OF FLYING THAT TRIGGERED MY **BREAKDOWN** BECAME A METAPHOR FOR ALL MY FEARS, NOW WILDLY OUT OF CONTROL

FEAR

HATE

DOUBT

FLYING FAILURE RIDICULE DEATH

* PSYCHO MAN © MARVEL COMICS (IN A BETTER WORLD, © JACK KIRBY) - EV

CONTROL... IS A **KEY** ISSUE HERE. I CAN'T CONTROL THE WAY THE WORLD WORKS-- ANY MORE THAN I CAN CONTROL AN AIRPLANE OR MY OWN EMOTIONAL WELL-BEING. IN THE REAL WORLD I AM **WEAK**, FLAWED AND **OVERWHELMED**.

BUT WHEN I DO MY COMICS-- I AM A **GOD**.

GOD

DUH-HAH!

I'M ONE WITH STUPID

A SLOPPY, **UNFOCUSED** AND **HALF-ASSED** GOD, PERHAPS-- BUT A GOD NONETHELESS. WHAT I SAY **GOES**.

D OF COURSE, NOW EVEN **THAT** S BEEN TAKEN AWAY FROM ME.

DRAW US! WE WANT TO HAVE MORE FUN!

I-- I CAN'T!

LORD OF THE DUNCE

YOU SUCK, "GOD"!

IT'S LIKE... SUBCONSCIOUSLY I DON'T FEEL LIKE I DESERVE **HAPPINESS** OR **SUCCESS** SO I CREATE THESE PETTY "**WOE IS ME**" **BULLSHIT PROBLEMS** TO DRAG ME DOWN... I MEAN--

-- WHAT WOULD I DO IF I EVER HAD TO FACE A REAL... **UH** ... TRAGEDY OR-- UM...

SELF-HATE

SELF-DOUBT

WHY DID YOU **STOP**?

BEN COOPER

PSYCHO BOY

I'M SORRY--

-- THE, UH, **TELEPROMPTER** WENT DOWN-- I DON'T REMEMBER MY NEXT **LINE**...

GIN MAKES A MAN

SHIT! CUT! CUT TO **COMMERCIAL**!

THIS COMIC STRIP HAS BEEN BROUGHT TO YOU BY:

KRAFFT-EBBING MACARONI & CHEESE DINNER

KRAFFT-EBBING MACARONI AND CHEESE - ORGASMICALLY CREAMY!! ABERRANT SHAPES!!

AND:

LUDDITE.COM

"COMING TO THE INTERNET JUST AS SOON AS WE FIGURE A FEW THINGS OUT"

AND:

WELL-BUTRIN

TRA-ZODONE

LORAZ-EPAM

THE NEUROTIC CARTOONIST'S FRIENDS!

, HE SHOULDN'T E RIPPED THESE I MEAN, THIS UFF ISN'T **ALL** THAT BAD!

HMM... IT'S NO GREAT **LOSS**, REALLY.

ARE YOU **MAD**?!

THIS IS $ DOWN THE DRAIN!!

NO, THIS IS **PALLIATIVE CLAPTRAP DOWN THE DRAIN**... AN UNEASY MIX OF **JUNK CULTURE** REFERENCES, **SELF-INDULGENT HISTRIONICS**, HALF-TRUTHS AND OUTRIGHT LIES--

YEAH, WELL, WASN'T IT PICASSO WHO SAID "ART IS A **LIE** THAT TELLS THE **TRUTH**?"

YEAH, **WELL**-- WASN'T IT **BUSY ARNOLD** WHO SAID--

"**COMICS ARE A LIE THAT SELLS MORE COMICS.**"

MY PARENTS DIVORCED WHEN I WAS THREE.
MY FATHER HAD VIRTUALLY NOTHING TO DO WITH US AFTER THE DIVORCE... EVEN THOUGH HE ONLY LIVED SEVERAL BLOCKS AWAY.
HE WAS A COLD AND INSENSITIVE MAN... TWO TRAITS HE PASSED ON TO ME ALONG WITH SOME TOYS AND COMICS.
I THINK MY MOTHER MARRIED HIM LARGELY TO GET OUT OF THE HOUSE --WHICH SEEMED TO BE THE CASE OF ALL THE OTHER YOUNG DIVORCEES MY MOM KNEW IN THE GOD-AWFUL, SHIT-BROWN UGLY 70'S I GREW UP IN.
@☆#!! PIGS!!
:SNIF:
HAPPY NOW?!
AND YOU'LL CLEAN THAT ROOM IF IT MEANS YOU STAY UP ALL @☆#! NIGHT!
THESE WOMEN GREW UP DURING T REPRESSIVE '50'S AND ENTERED IN SHITTY RELATIONSHIPS TO ESCAP THEIR SUFFOCATING SURROUNDINGS A FUCKED-UP PARENTS, ONLY TO FIND THEMSELVES RAISING KIDS ON THEIR OWN WITH LITTLE MONEY OR SUPPOR ADDING TO A CONFUSED RAGE AND FRUSTRATION THAT WOULD BE FOIST ONTO THEIR BEWILDERED CHILDRE
MONSTER TIMES
SPIDER MAN
MY MOTHER WORKED HARD AS A LEGAL SECRETARY TO MAKE ENDS MEET, OFTEN TAKING FILES HOME TO TYPE UP AT NIGHT IN OUR SHITTY, ROACH-INFESTED APARTMENT IN BROOKLYN.
CLACK CLACK CLACK CLACKITY CLACK
I'D OFTEN LIE AWAKE IN THE MIDDLE OF THE NIGHT, LISTENING TO THE TYPEWRITER KEYS SOUNDING LIKE ANGRY GIANT METAL INSECTS TRYING TO TEAR THE BUILDING APART.
MY MOTHER TRIED TO BE THERE FOR ME... BUT I WAS A DIFFICU KID TO HAVE, AND RESPONSIBILITIES AND FRUSTRATIONS OVERWHELMED HER. SO, WITH NO ONE TO CONNECT TO, I FOUND MY OW FOSTER PARENTS TO FILL IN THE BLANKS MY FAMILY LEFT ALL AROUND
I LOVE YOU
LET ME TELL YOU A STORY
I WAS, MORE THAN I CARE TO ADMIT--AND ALONG WITH FAR TOO MANY OTHER DAMAGED KIDS--RAISED BY TELEVISION, BY COMIC BOOKS, AND BY THE MOVIE SCREEN. POP CULTURE PAVED MY ESCAPIST ROUTE FROM THE LOUSY WORLD AROUND ME
I HAD MY OWN BIG-LITTLE WORLD OF SUPERHEROES AND SUPERVILLAINS, MONSTERS AND ALIENS, TALKING ANIMALS AND DETECTIVES, SPACE MEN AND KNIGHTS IN ARMOR...
I COULD VISIT OZ AND CAMELOT AND SHERWOOD FOREST AND THE SHIRE AND ALTAIR IV AND SKULL ISLAND AND ASGAR AND THE BAXTER BUILDING AND WONDER LAND AND SLUMBERLAND AND PEPPERLAN
AND THEY WERE ALL BETTE PLACES THAN BROOKLYN, WIT ITS BULLIES AND RACISTS AN COCKROACHES AND SCREAMIN AND CRYING PARENTS...
THE INCREDIBLE
UNFORTUNATELY, ALL THOSE YEARS OF CATHODE FOSTER CARE PRETTY MUCH SCRAMBLED MY BRAINS AS MUCH AS MY REAL FAMILY DID--BECAUSE THEY HARDWIRED ME FOR A WORLD OF DISAPPOINTMENT. THEY TOLD ME THAT GOOD TRIUMPHED OVER EVIL, HARD WORK PAID OFF, AND THAT IF YOU PLAYED BY THE RULES YOU'D COME OUT ON TOP.
AND I--A DUMB-FUCK KNOW-NOTHI KID, A BLANK EMOTIONAL SLATE EAG FOR SOMEONE'S TRUTH TO BE WRIT ACROSS IT--GOT SUCKERED. I FEL FOR IT ALL, HOOK, LINE AND ZINGE
THEY TOLD ME THAT WOMEN WERE BEAUTIFUL AND VIRTUOUS.
THAT MEN WERE NOBLE AND STRONG.
THAT FAMILIES LOVED ONE ANOTHER.
AURORA PERFECT FAMILY MODEL KIT
TESTORS
REPORT CARD A+
HOW TO BUILD Y PERFECT FAM
AND THAT EVERYTHING WOULD WORK OUT IN THE LAST REEL, THE LAST PAGE... THE LAST PANEL.

UT IT WAS ALL
LLSHIT. THEY
IED TO ME.
HELL, I DON'T BLAME ANYONE. I LIE FOR A LIVING MYSELF.
ROMANCE
ITTY REPARTEE
SE FAMILIES
IOUS ENEMIES
TIC LOCALES
CONTRIVANCES
SNAPPY DIALOGUE
HAPPY ENDINGS
LOVE CONQUERS ALL
STOCK CHARACTERS
BUT HOLLYWOOD AND ITS VINES FUCKED UP MY IDEA OF WHAT THE WORLD WAS REALLY LIKE WITH THEIR 31 FLAVORS OF SUGAR-COATED SNAKE OIL.
EVEN WORSE-- THEY FUCKED UP MY IDEA OF WHAT THE WORLD OF MAKE-BELIEVE WAS LIKE. I WAS LED TO BELIEVE THAT THE ENTERTAINMENT INDUSTRY WAS A PLACE WHERE TALENTED, HAPPY AND HONEST CRAFTSMEN AND WOMEN WORKED TOGETHER LIKE CHEERFUL ELVES TO BRING US DREAMS.
NOW STAY TUNED FOR "FANTASY ISLAND!"
LET'S GO FOLKS!
OH BOY!
HOORAY FOR HOLLYWOOD!
A RAISE FOR EVERY ONE
MR PRODUCER
PROPS
SCRIPT
THAT WAS THE OTHER BIG LIE.
I GOT OLDER I LEARNED THAT THE PEOPLE WHO SAW ME THROUGH MY CHILDHOOD RE JUST THAT-- PEOPLE. THEY WERE NOT GIANTS. THEY WERE RARELY HEROES. AND RST OF ALL, FEW OF THEM POSSESSED THE VIRTUES OF THEIR GRANDIOSE CREATIONS.
DEAL
VARIETY ACTRESS CAST IN ROLE
CARTOON SCRIPT
PINK SLIP
PINK SLIP
ER-PAY NO ATTENTION TO THE ENTERTAINMENT INDUSTRY BEHIND THE CURTAIN!!
I HAVE ONLY MYSELF TO BLAME FOR MY NAIVE ILLUSIONS. BECAUSE I WANTED TO BELIEVE IN A WORLD THAT MADE SENSE, ENDED HAPPILY, AND FIT THE RUNNING TIME JUST RIGHT.
UF!
UF!
EVAN'Z 2OAP BOX
HELP!
SNEY WAS AN ANTI-SEMITE. LEWIS CARROLL LUSTED AFTER UNDERAGE RABBIT HOLES, AND D DAMN IT-- GOD DAMN IT! STAN AND JACK WEREN'T "SMILIN" OR "JOLLY" OR EVEN FRIENDS!
D I FOOLED MYSELF INTO THINKING I COULD KE SOME SENSE OF THE WORLD BY CREATING OWN WORLD-- THAT I COULD BE HAPPY IF I ST MADE UP THINGS THAT WOULD MAKE ME HAPPY.
I KNOW!
COMICS AND MOVIES MAKE ME HAPPY-- MAYBE MY COMICS WILL MAKE OTHER PEOPLE HAPPY-- AND THEY'LL LIKE ME AND THEN I'LL BE REALLY HAPPY!
DUH-HAH!
FREE!
#1 EVAN'S COMICS
"SO HE MADE THINGS UP AND THEY MADE HIM ABOUT AS HAPPY AS HE'D EVER BEEN."
BUT NOW THE THINGS I MAKE UP ARE A CLUTTERED MESS...
MUZMO
UNDEROOS
... BECAUSE I'M A CLUTTERED MESS.
AND MY COMICS HAVE BECOME PATHETIC SELF-SERVING MESSAGES IN BOTTLES SCATTERED ACROSS THE WORLD... CHEAPLY PRINTED LITTLE CRIES FOR ATTENTION BEGGING SOMEONE TO ACKNOWLEDGE MY PITIFUL EXISTANCE--
DORK
MILK AND CHEES
YOU RANG?
HECTIC PLANET
--PLEADING WITH SOMEONE TO REMEMBER ME AFTER I'M NOTHING BUT WORM FOOD AND SHIT AND DUST...
Y WORK LOST AND FORGOTTEN IN ATTICS D LANDFILLS AND THE QUARTER BINS OF HE LAST FEW DINOSAUR COMIC SHOPS--
COMICS?! UGH!
BUSINES SALE
WORLD'S FUNNEST
25¢ FOR 4 MONTHS OF SOMEONE'S LIFE
FOOM
DORK SEVEN
THIS PILE FREE!
--YELLOWED AND TATTERED MEMENTOS F NOTHING MORE THAN JUST ANOTHER PRETENTIOUS, SELF-IMPORTANT, SELF-OBSESSED, SELF-ABSORBED PARASITE.
ANOTHER NEEDY, NERDY MIDDLE-CLASS WHINER WITH SOME ART SUPPLIES AND A COMPUTER WHO WAS SCARED AND CONFUSED BUT DIDN'T HAVE THE INSIGHT OR TALENT TO SAY ANYTHING NEW ABOUT FEAR OR CONFUSION.
DUNCE
A LOUD, USELESS, REDUNDANT KNOW-NOTHING WHO FINALLY DRIED UP AND BLEW AWAY...
... A DROP IN THE JUNK-CULTURE BUCKET.
A BLIP ON THE HIPNESS RADAR.
EVAN DORKINS 1965-1999 "HE MADE JOKE BOOKS" BIG SHIT
DORK
FIGHT MAN
BILL AND TED'S
SUPERGIRL
INSTANT PIANO
A COG IN THE BULLSHIT MACHINE.

DO YOU REALLY BELIEVE ALL OF THAT?

I DON'T KNOW.
I HONESTLY DON'T KNOW.

WHAT DOES IT MATTER WHAT I BELIEVE... OR WHAT I THINK... ALL THAT MATTERS IS WHAT I FEEL!
AND WHAT DOES EVEN THAT MEAN? I JUST TALK AND TALK ...NOTHING EVER GETS RESOLVED.
NOTHING EVER MEANS ANYTHING.
IT'S ALL JUST SHIT.

LOOK, UH, CAN I JUST WRITE YOU A CHECK NOW?
I REALLY DON WANT TO TALK ABOUT THIS ANYMORE.

SCHWA

MY GOD...
...HOW CAN YOU STAND TO LISTEN TO THAT WHINY IDIOT DAY IN AND DAY OUT?

I CAN BARELY STAND IT FOR AN HOUR A WEEK--
--AND I'M GETTING PAID!
WELL... WHAT CAN I TELL YOU?

HE MAKES ME LAUGH.

HA HA HA

HA HA HA
POSS TITLE?
CLUTTERED (LIKE MY HEAD)
CALL JOEY- RE: LIS! 98-99
IS BOLLAND'S COVER IN YET?!
evan dorkin
THE LAST LAFF?!
HA HA

A FEW WORDS ABOUT THAT LAST STORY ...

"WHAT DOES IT LOOK LIKE I'M DOING?" WAS ORIGINALLY PRODUCED IN 1995 FOR THE FOURTH AND FINAL ISSUE OF the INSTANT PIANO ANTHOLOGY.

THE INITIAL IDEA BEHIND THE STRIP WAS TO COMBINE SCRIPTED GAG MATERIAL WITH LINKING SEQUENCES THAT WOULD BE IMPROVISED ON THE PAGE.

ONE UNEXPECTED OUTCOME OF THAT LITTLE EXPERIMENT WAS THE INTRODUCTION OF AUTOBIOGRAPHICAL ELEMENTS INTO THE STORY.

WHERE THE HELL DID YOU COME FROM?

THOSE ELEMENTS BEING MY THEN GROWING ANXIETIES ABOUT LIFE, DEATH, WORK AND THE POSSIBLE COLLAPSE OF THE COMIC BOOK INDUSTRY.

WHEN I DECIDED TO REPRINT THE STRIP IN DORK #7 IN 1999, I REALIZED THAT I'D NEED TO ADDRESS SOME OF THE ISSUES I'D RAISED BEFORE PULLING MY DURANTE ACT.

THIS LED TO THE CREATION OF "CLUTTERED, LIKE MY HEAD," INITIALLY CONCEIVED OF AS A RESPONSE STRIP THAT WOULD FILL READERS IN ON WHERE MY HEAD HAD BEEN DURING THE PREVIOUS FOUR YEARS.

AS YOU COULD TELL, I WAS IN PRETTY BAD SHAPE. NOT SO MUCH WHEN I WROTE AND DREW IT, BUT LET'S JUST SAY THAT FROM 1996 TO 1998 LIFE WASN'T MUCH OF A PARTY.

I FULLY INTENDED TO EXAMINE MY BREAKDOWN IN "CLUTTERED"-- WHAT CAME AS A SURPRISE DURING THE PROCESS WAS THE MATERIAL DEALING WITH MY CHILDHOOD AND MY LOVE/HATE RELATIONSHIP WITH POP CULTURE AND MY PLACE IN IT.

FILL ME WITH BRILLIANCE. NOW.
HEY! HEY! I'M TALKING TO YOU!

BUT THE BIGGEST SURPRISE WAS THE REACTION TO DORK #7. I EXPECTED SOME FOLKS TO HATE IT, AS IT WASN'T EXACTLY A STRAIGHTFORWARD GAG BOOK.

FUCK YOU, DORKIN! WHERE ARE THE LAUGHS?! YOU PUT OUT ANOTHER ISSUE LIKE THIS DORK #7 CRAP AND I'LL READ IT IN THE STORE AND NOT BUY IT!! *
MY FAN

*ACTUAL THREAT BY ACTUAL ASSHOLE - EV

FOR THE MOST PART, HOWEVER, THE RESPONSE WAS ENTHUSIASTIC AND SUPPORTIVE. I RECEIVED OVER 200 LETTERS, SOME DEEPLY PERSONAL, SOME PRACTICALLY CONFESSIONAL.

HOLY SHIT.
AND I THOUGHT I HAD A LOUSY CHILDHOOD.

I CAN'T TELL YO HOW MANY OF TH WERE FROM FELLO CARTOONISTS. WE REALLY ARE ONE QUIETLY FUCKED-UP BUNCH

HOORAY! CLAP CLA
ME SOMEDAY

DON'T YOU THINK IT'S IRONIC THAT YOUR COMIC ABOUT HAVING PROBLEMS WITH ATTENTION AND EXPECTATIONS BRINGS YOU YET MORE ATTENTION AND STRONGER EXPECTATIONS FOR YOUR SUBSEQUENT WORK?

NEXT PANEL, PLEASE!

WHICH BRINGS US TO THE MOST PREVALENT QUESTIO READERS HAVE ASKED ME SINCE I PUT DORK #7 OU

CAN YOU FLY?

ARE YOU OKAY?

WAS THAT PHONE SEX STORY TRUE

WHEN ARE YOU GONNA DO ANOTHER MILK AND CHEESE?

WHAT THE FUCK IS "HYDRA"?

NO, REALLY. ARE YOU OKAY?

① I'VE GOTTEN ON AIRPLANES AGAIN, BUT I CAN'T SAY I LOVE FLYING, ESPECIALLY POST-9/11. ② I'M OKAY. ③ SADLY, ALL THE AUTIOBIO ELEMENTS IN THE STORY ARE FACTUAL. ④ NO COMMENT. ⑤ BELIEVE ME, YOU DON'T WANT TO KNOW.

⑥ OKAY, LOOK, I'LL NEVER BE THE POSTER BOY FOR EMOTIONAL STABILITY. I STILL SUFFER FROM BOUTS OF ANXIETY, BUT THEY'RE A FAR CRY FROM THE TEXAS DEATH MATCHES I USED TO GET BOOKED INTO. MY COMICS ARE STILL CLUTTERED, BUT MY HEAD IS LESS SO, NOWADAYS.

THAT LINE IS TERRIBLE.
I LIKE IT. FUCK OFF.
REMEMBER WHAT THALBERG SAID!

ANYWAY, LET'S NOT END THING ON A DOWNER. WE'VE GOT A LITTLE SUPPLEMENTAL SECTI UP NEXT FOR YOU, WITH COVER GALLERY AND SOME STRIPS COLORED BY SARA AMONG OTHER ODDS AND END SO DON'T WORRY ABOUT ME NONE, OK? I'M ALL RIGHT!

SMILES, EVERYONE! SMILE

for the LOVE of GOD
evan/00
NOW THIS IS NOT WIDELY KNOWN, BUT ABOUT EVERY SEVEN DECADES OR SO, GOD FALLS HARD FOR A MORTAL WOMAN...
HERE WE GO AGAIN!
SEE? SEE HER?!
THAT'S THE ONE I WAS TELLING YOU ABOUT-- WITH THE STOMACH!
EARTH
NICE BIT OF ADAM'S RIB THERE, EH?
...AND NOTHING IN HEAVEN OR ON EARTH CAN DENY HIM FROM SCRATCHING THESE SEVENTY YEAR ITCHES.
THIS TIME AROUND, GOD HAD BECOME INFATUATED WITH A TWENTY-TWO YEAR OLD FASHION MODEL FROM PARAMUS, NEW JERSEY.
FROM THE BIG G
uhh, well. I'm very flattered...
BUT, UH, LOOK --I'M LIKE, REALLY NOT INTO OLDER GUYS, OKAY? AND RELIGION'S LIKE, A TOTAL TURN-OFF FOR ME!
AND, UH, I'VE GOT THIS SHOOT IN TWENTY MINUTES, SO I REALLY HAVE TO GO NOW!
TAXI! POLICE!?
I ♥ NY
BUT SHE SPURNED HIS ADVANCES, BEING QUITE THE LAPSED CATHOLIC.
THIS MADE GOD ONLY WANT HER MORE, TO THE POINT OF OBSESSION.
GOD, I'M HORNY.
OR IS THAT, "ME, I'M HORNY"?
OH, FAH! THINK I'LL GO ERUPT A VOLCANO.
GOD THEN BEGAN TO STALK THE GIRL, BECOMING AN OMNIPRESENCE IN HER LIFE, WATCHING OVER HER EVERY WAKING HOUR.
AUG
SEPT 2
SEPT 9
REALIZING A RESTRAINING ORDER WOULD BE POINTLESS, SHE FINALLY RELENTED AND AGREED TO A DATE WITH GOD.
THAT EVENING, GOD PLEDGED HIS DEVOTION TO HER, PROMISING TO DO ANYTHING SHE ASKED IF SHE WOULD ONLY BE HIS.
TINK
SHE JOKINGLY ASKED GOD TO KILL THE CAREERS OF ALL THE WAYANS BROTHERS. GOD INSTANTLY MADE THEM JANITORS. THIS IMPRESSED AND DELIGHTED THE GIRL.

AFTER DINNER, ONE THING LED TO ANOTHER, AND THEY ENDED UP IN A CLOUDBED TOGETHER.
OH GOD!
OH GOD!
OH GOD!

THEY BEGAN SEEING ONE ANOTHER, AND FOR A WHILE IT WAS HEAVENLY. BUT SOON THEIR RELATIONSHIP BEGAN TO DETERIORATE AS THEY GOT TO KNOW ONE ANOTHER BETTER.
--HE'S JUST SO OVERBEARING AND SOOO FULL OF HIMSELF! ALL HE EVER DOES IS TALK ABOUT HIMSELF AND HIS WORK, IT'S ALWAYS, "LOOK WHAT I DID," "LOOK WHAT I MADE," "COULD THE STARS BE ANY GRANDER," BLAH BLAH BLAH!
I JUST CAN'T STAND HIS POMPOUS ASS ANY MORE!

NOTHING PLEASES THAT WOMAN! I'VE DONE ALL SHE'S ASKED! BANNED SUV'S, SAVED THE RAIN FORESTS, CURED ACNE-- I EVEN LET HER HELP CREATE LIFE ON OTHER PLANET
BUT IT'S NEVER ENOU
ALL SHE DOES IS COMPL
"THE CHURCH IS CORRUP
"JESUS DOESN'T LIKE M
BLAH BLAH BLAH! THA
WITCH IS DRVING ME MA

FINALLY, ONE FATEFUL DAY, EVERYTHING CAME TO A HEAD.
AND ANOTHER THING--I WANT YOU TO REVEAL YOUR EXISTENCE TO THE WORLD! I'M TIRED OF BEING A KEPT WOMAN!
VOGUE

DAMN YOU WOMAN! THIS TIME YOU GO TOO FAR!!
eep.

REALIZING ONLY TOO LATE WHAT HE'D DONE, G
COULD ONLY WATCH AS SHE FELL AWAY FROM HEAVE
BUT-
OH, BIG MA
MR. ALMIGH
SEND A GIR
TO HELL JUS
TO SHUT HER
VOGUE
FINE! HAVE IT YOUR WAY! I'D RATHER BURN THAN BE WITH YOU!

ALL IN ALL, GOD TOOK THE BREAK-UP WELL. HE FLOODED BANGLADESH, GAVE HIS EX'S MOTHER CERVICAL CANCER, AND SWORE OFF MORTALS.
YET AGAIN.
DEATH TOLL 342

SPEAKING OF HIS EX... UPON HER ARRIVAL IN HELL THE DEVIL TOOK ONE LOOK AT HER AND PROMPTLY FELL HEAD OVER HOOVES IN LOVE WITH HER. AND SHE WITH HIM.
AS OF THIS WRITING THE TWO CONTINUE TO LIVE IN SIN--
DADDY'S LITTLE DEVIL
--AND ARE EXPECTIN
THEIR THIRD ANTI
CHRIST ANY DAY NO

finis-

Fisher-Price Theatre Presents:
George Orwell's
1984

Adapted by
Evan Dorkin
& Sarah Dyer

WHAT HAVE WE LEARNED FROM GEORGE ORWELL'S 1984?

1. Ignorance really is strength. 2. Two minutes of hate is never enough.
3. Setting a dystopian society only 35 years into the future is ungood.

ROCK PAPER SCISSORS

ROCK BREAKS SCISSORS.
OW!
SNAP!

SCISSORS CUTS PAPER.
AAA!

PAPER COVERS ROCK.
CRINKLE!

ROCK RUPTURES PAPER.
RIP!
YEARGH!

SCISSORS DEFENESTRATES ROCK.
MASH!
AAAAA!

PAPER SUFFOCATES SCISSORS.
MMPH!
MMPH!

PAPER THROWS LIT M-80 AT ROCK.
AHH!
BOOM!

ROCK HEADBUTTS PAPER.
CRUMPLE!
OOF!

PAPER KICKS ROCK IN GROIN.
OOF!

SCISSORS AND ROCK TEAR PAPER TO PIECES.

PAPER GETS FRIENDS TO GANG UP ON ROCK AND SCISSORS.

ROCK AND SCISSORS SET PAPER'S FRIENDS ON FIRE.
GAS

PAPER SPREADS RUMOR THAT ROCK AND SCISSORS ARE GAY LOVERS.
?
?
HA
HA HA

ROCK SUES PAPER.
?
PAPER
$$$

SCISSORS SUES PAPER.
PAPER
$$$
!

PAPER COUNTERSUES ROCK AND SCISSORS.
OH YEAH?
?!!
SAME TO YOU!
$
$

PAPER TRIES TO MAKE A DEAL WITH SCISSORS.
SST-
SST!
!

ROCK BREAKS SCISSORS.
SNAP!
AARGH!

SCISSORS SACRIFICES PAPER TO SATAN

PAPER THROWS ACID IN SCISSOR'S FACE.
AARGH!
SSSSS!

ROCK, SCISSORS AND PAPER GET INTO BRAWL ON LIVE TELEVISION TALK SHOW.
BLEEP!

PAPER USES INFLUENTIAL POLITICAL AND MEDIA CONTACTS TO MALIGN ROCK AND SCISSORS.
ROCK AND SCISSORS MENACE TO SOCIETY

ROCK ORGANIZES STREET GANGS AND MERCENARIES INTO PRIVATE ARMY.

SCISSORS UNITES ANTI-GOVERNMENT MILITIA MEN AND CULTISTS INTO TERRORIST STRIKE FORCE.

PAPER CALLS FOR STATE OF EMERGENCY AND MARTIAL LAW.
HUP
HUP!
!

ROCK ORDERS HIS TROOPS TO TAKE THE STREETS.

SCISSORS COUNTERS WITH A BIO-CHEMICAL CAMPAIGN OF TERROR.

GOVERNMENT SHOOTS TROOPS.
TROOPS BOMB GOVERNMENT.
ANTHRAX KILLS EVERYONE.

FIN

CARTOONIST goes to HELL!

THE WORLD
THE FLESH
AND THE DEVIL PUPPET

NEW AND USED

DID YOU HEAR ABOUT THE USED RECORD STORE ON FOURTH AND WILSON? THEY HAVE THIS REALLY INTERESTING TRADE-IN OFFER.

HEARTBREAK HOTEL RECORDS
CDS · TAPES · NEW AND USED VINYL
RECORDS
WILSO
OPEN

BASICALLY, YOU CAN BRING IN ALL THE MUSIC YOU OWN THAT YOU CAN'T BEAR TO HEAR ANYMORE BECAUSE IT REMINDS YO OF YOUR EX-BOYFRIEND OR EX-GIRLFRIEND

NEW
JOY DIVISION
CONNIE FRANCIS
LEONARD COHEN
ROY ORBISO
PATSY CLINE ONLY
HANK WILLIAMS
BILLIE HOLIDA BOX 2

IN RETURN, THEY'LL GIVE YOU STORE CREDIT TOWARDS NEW MUSIC HAND-PICKED TO CHEER YOU UP AND HELP YOU FORGET THE BREAK-UP.

OPEN
PUFFY AMI YUMI
ALLAN SHERMAN
MY SON THE FOLKSINGER
EDITH PIAF
SPIKE JONES

I HEAR BUSINESS IS GOOD. BUT KEEP THIS IN MIND-- YOU'RE ON YOUR OWN WHEN IT COMES TO YOUR MIXED TAPES

NOBODY WANTS THOSE ANYMORE.
XTC
LULU TO SIR WITH LOVE
NICK CAVE AND THE BAD SEEDS
SMITHS
TOM WAITS
JOY DIVISI
REPLACEM

EVAN 6/01

WE ALL DIE ALONE.
Rx
XXX
ROTGUT
100%
PROOF

COMICS ARE DEAD!
THE
COMICS
JOURNAL
THEY DESERVED IT!
THE MAGAZINE OF COMICS NEWS-
-AND CRITICISM! (NO, REALLY!)
#214 $5.95 U.S. $7.95 CAN
MEANWHILE, AT THE BOTTOM OF THE BARREL...
BLAH BLAH @☆#! COMICS %$¢$ RETAILERS BLAH ☆#@! FANS #%*! EVERYONE etc etc
SHUT UP YOU BABY!
YOU'RE NOT FUNNY!
MILK
ACTION GIRL
evan '99 sarah
SLG

ev-
BURN IN
HELL

MURDER CAN BE FUN!

(FOR TWO DOLLARS AND NINETY-FIVE CENTS) issue #1

DISASTER FILLED FIRST ISSUE!

THE PORT CHICAGO EXPLOSION!

THE TRIANGLE SHIRTWAIST FIRE!

THE GREAT BOSTON MOLASSES FLOOD!

EVAN DORKIN

SLAVE LABOR GRAPHICS

DORK
NUMBER SEVEN
$2.95
S.L.G.
?
?
COMICS
BY EVAN DORK N
"Read 'Em A Weep!"
– says Mr. Chimpie
DORK #7

$3.50
SLG
DORK
SMILES, EVERYONE, SMILES
evan
-00-

DORK
ISSUE #9 PRICE-$2.95
SLAVE LABOR GRAPHICS
YOU THINK THIS IS FUNNY ?
I AM CULPABLE.
I KNOW WHEN YOU DIE.
EVAN DORKIN -01-
DISCO BALL

COMICS
DORK
number ten
ANK
$2.95
SLG
Please

DORK

"COMEDY"

"TRAGEDY"

number SEVEN

DORK
IS PUBLISHED BY
SLAVE LABOR GRAPHICS
DAN VADO – OWNER
BOB SIMPKINS - MANAGER
TRAVIS O'NEIL - SLUGGER
CRAIG PAPE - HALL OF FAME
SEE AD IN BACK FOR FREE CATALOG INFORMATION

by
evan dorkin
po box 060380
staten island
N.Y. 10306
evandorkin@aol.com

I EXPECT NOTHING. YOU SHOULD, TOO.

COVER COLORS AND EDITORIAL AID - SARAH DYER

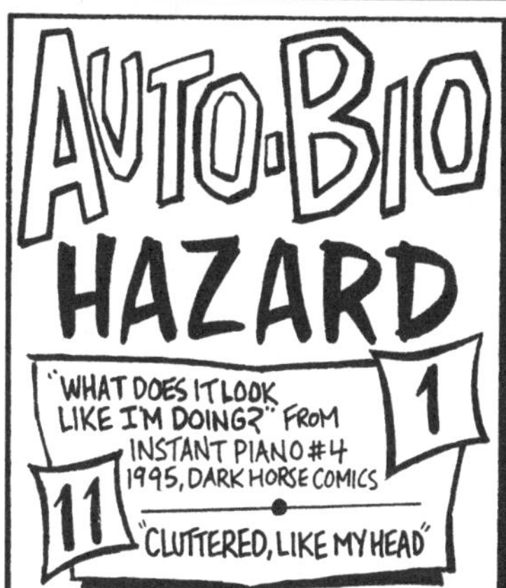

THIS IS THE LAST TIME, I SWEAR!
PAYOLA

AUTO-BIO HAZARD
"WHAT DOES IT LOOK LIKE I'M DOING?" FROM INSTANT PIANO #4 1995, DARK HORSE COMICS

"CLUTTERED, LIKE MY HEAD"

I KNOW, IT'S LATE, I'M SORRY.

VISIT THE HOUSE OF FUN
www.houseoffun.com

"WE PROMISE TO UPDATE IT SOMEDAY"

OBLIGATORY DORK 7 PLAYLIST

PORTISHEAD · PORTISHEAD
COYLE & SHARPE · ON THE LOOSE
BUZZCOCKS · SINGLES GOING STEADY
FRANK McCOURT · ANGELA'S ASHES AUDIO BK.
ELMER BERNSTEIN · SWEET SMELL OF SUCCESS
THE AQUABATS · RETURN OF/FURY OF
DEVO · FREEDOM OF CHOICE
X · BEYOND AND BACK
XTC · BIG EXPRESS
WFMU · 91.1 FM

UPCOMING!

SEPT - MILK & CHEESE METAL LUNCHBOX FROM DHC
OCT - 3 PG COLOR ELTINGVILLE STRIP IN WIZARD MAGAZINE
- NEW EPISODES OF SGC2C AND BATMAN BEYOND by SARAH & I
- THE SEQUEL TO OUR SUPERGIRL ADVENTURES DC COMIC - WORLD'S FUNNEST IN 2000!!

HOW TO GET SUED: PART 5

ONE HAND UP MY ASS!
AH AH
AH AH

HOW TO GET SUED: PART 6

HULK SMASHED!
XXX

BLESS ME, FATHER... IT'S BEEN EIGHT MONTHS SINCE I'VE LAST DRAWN A COMIC STRIP.

MY GOD, YOU SUCK!
AND YOU'RE NOT CATHOLIC. SO BEAT IT YOU KIKE BASTARD!
DORK 7

NEXT ISSUE!! LESS TEXT! NO ANGST! AND MORE DUMB GAGS LIKE THIS:

EXCUSE ME, MISS?
DATE RAPE FOR DUMMIES
MISS?!

THE BORING SHIT!

CWP

SLG

FIRST PRINTING AUG '99 PRINTED IN CANADA

--BUT FIRST...A FEW WORDS REGARDING DORK #7
HEY--I JUST WANTED TO THANK EVERYONE WHO WROTE IN ABOUT THE LAST ISSUE. I CAN'T ANSWER ALL OF MY MAIL ANYMORE--AND I'VE RECEIVED NEARLY 200 LETTERS ON DORK #7 SO FAR (!), SO I THOUGHT I'D USE THIS SPACE TO SAY "THANKS" FOR THE RESPONSE, AND THAT I'M SORRY I COULDN'T WRITE BACK TO EVERYONE.
SO WHAT?
WHO CARES?
YAWN!
AND NOW, ONTO THE NEW ISSUE, WHICH, DEPENDING ON YOUR PERSPECTIVE IS EITHER A RETURN TO FORM, OR A STEP BACKWARDS IN MY "MATURATION AS AN ARTIST."
OH, IF YOU HADN'T HEARD: I'M CURRENTLY WORKING ON AN ELTINGVILLE CLUB PILOT FOR THE CARTOON NETWORK. I'M AS SHOCKED BY THIS AS YOU ARE.
COMING IN NOVEMBER! WORLD'S FUNNEST from DC COMICS, MY SCRIPT, ART BY DAVID MAZZUCCHELLI, JAIME HERNANDEZ, DAVE GIBBONS, ETAL!
THANKS TO DARK HORSE COMICS FOR THE NOD TO PRINT THE SCATTER BRAIN STRIPS EARLY (PGS 11-13)
FROM SLG- MILK AND CHEESE BEER MUGS + BOWLING SHIRTS! STEEE-RIKE!!
THANKS TO JOHN MARR FOR LETTING ME RUN THE MCBF STRIPS!
HA HA HA! OH, HOW DROLL!
I DUNNO WHEN DORK #9 WILL BE OUT.
"IF DORK #8 IS ANYTHING LIKE THAT DORK #7 BULLSHIT, I'M GONNA READ IT IN THE SHOP AND NOT BUY IT! SO FUCK YOU, DORKIN!"
"OH MY GOD--DORK #7 WAS SO AMAZING! JUST PLEASE DON'T KILL YOURSELF, O.K? BUT--IF YOU REALLY HAVE TO, COULD YOU SEND ME SOME ARTWORK FIRST?"
DORK
FOOM
and now...
DORK 8
by evan dorkin
po box 060380
staten island ny 10306
evandorkin@aol.com
"AHHH, I LIKED YOUR STUFF BETTER WHEN NOBODY LIKED YOUR STUFF."
"MMPH! MVUMUM! MFFMM!"
"I THOUGHT DORK #7 WAS YOUR BEST WORK! BUT I'M A CRAPPY DRAWING, SO WHAT THE FUCK DO I KNOW?"
"WHAT THE HELL IS A DORK #7?"
VILLAGE OF THE DAMNED COMICS & MODELS
PREVIEWS
DER LEGAL CRAP
SLG
DORK IS PUBLISHED ONCE IN A WHILE BY SLAVE LABOR GRAPHICS. CONTENTS © 2000 evandorkin. ANY SIMILARITY TO PERSONS LIVING OR DEAD AS NAILS IS A COINCIDENCE, I SWEAR! OR AN ATTEMPT AT SATIRE, HONEST! NO PART OF THIS RAG MAY BE REPRODUCED W/O MY SAY SO--NO SHIT!
COLORS/SEPS/COMPUTER SMARTS and COMMON SENSE BY SARAH DYER
FOR MORE INFO ON WHAT IT IS WE DO, CHECK OUT OUR SITE: www.houseoffun.com
— DORK 8 OFFICIAL PLAYLIST —
AQUABATS-VS FLOATING EYE OF DEATH
PIXIES ALL/LUSH-GALA/PROPELLARHEADS-DECKS AND DRUMS.../BILLIE HOLIDAY-STANDARDS
STAN FREBERG-TIP OF THE FREBERG-WFMU
CWP
DAN VADO-ACE
BOB SIMPKINS-KING
TRAVIS O'NEIL-JACK OF CLUBS
FIRST PRINTING SEPT 2000 PRINTED IN CANA BY GHOSTS

DORA WILCOX: WORLD'S WORST DYKE
AHHH, FUCK!
NOT AGAIN!
K.D. LANG
ELISSA RIDGE
I WASN'T SPEEDING ON PURPOSE, OFFICER--I'M JUST NOT USED TO MY NEW SWEDISH CAR YET!
LOOK, PAL--DON'T YOU GIVE ME ANY GODDAM SAAB STORIES!
HOW TO GET SUED: PART 7
HI! I LIKE YOU! LET'S BE FRIENDS!
AND LET'S CUDDLE!
AND BATHE TOGETHER!
CASPER THE OVERLY FRIENDLY GHOST
DUNCE
DUH-HAW!
MARVEL COMICS RECESSION FUNNIES PART 2
YEAH, WELL, TIMES WERE TOUGH AFTER THE BANKRUPTCY, BUT, Y'KNOW, I ADAPTED.
GET BACK TO WORK!
BIG MAC
BIG MAC
GET IT? GET IT? NO? CHRIST, WHAT ARE YOU, FUCKING ILLITERATE?
--AND THIS VASE WAS ONCE OWNED BY THE CHINESE EMPEROR CHOW MEI FUN!
GOLLY!
BULL IN A CHINA SHOP
TABLET OF CONTENTS
PG1- YOU'RE SOAKING IN IT!
PG2- MONDO "FUN"! ENJOY!
PG7- "ADVERTISING CHARACTERS OF YESTERYEAR"
PG8- MURDER CAN BE FUN!
PG9- "FOR THE LOVE OF GOD"
PG11- FISHER PRICE THEATRE'S "1984"
PG13- ROCK, PAPER, SCISSORS
PG14- THE ELTINGVILLE CLUB IN- "UNSTABLE MOLECULES"
PG17- MORE MURDER CAN BE FUN
PG19- THE DEVIL PUPPETS INVISIBLE COLLEGE OF SECRET KNOWLEDGE
L.A. / N.Y.
HAVE A NICE DAY!
GINSENG
GINKO BILOBA
FUCK YOU!
FUCK YOU!
HEALTH BARN
HAVE A NICE DAY...
PORNO MOVIE WRAP PARTY
GOOD NIGHT, EVERYONE!
THANKS FOR COMING!
--THEN TAKE A GODDAM RIGHT ONTO MUD ROAD, AN' DRIVE FIVE FUCKIN' MILES OVER COCK-SUCKIN' MUD 'TIL Y'SEE THIS UGLY-ASS TREE WITH THIS HUGE PUSSY-LOOKIN' KNOT IN IT--YOU PULL LEFT AT THAT THERE SUMBITCH --AND YER ASSES ARE THERE, NO SHIT!
GAS
WES WOULD NEVER AGAIN ASK ANYONE FOR "EXPLICIT DIRECTIONS"
LOOKS LIKE THOSE EGYPTIANS WERE RIGHT!
AW, SHIT!
GLARF!
I NEVER SHOULD HAVE FILLED OUT THAT ORGAN DONOR CARD!
YO! BACK THE FUCK UP!
SECUR
NORTH POLE
DIDN'T YOU KNOW?! BUMBLES BOUNCE!

FEAR NOT!
IT'S HERE!
DORK
by evan dorkin, "YOUR FRIEND IN COMICS"
#9
P.O. BOX 06038
STATEN ISLAND
N.Y. 10306
EVANDORKIN@AOL.C
COVER COLORS / SEPS, PRE-PRESS AND SAVVY - MISS SARAH DYER
FOR MORE INFORMATION ON OUR COMICS & T.V. WORK, VISIT THE HOUSE OF FUN at WWW.HOUSEOFFUN.COM
HA HA HA HA
LOOK FOR US AT THIS YEAR'S (SMALL PRESS) EXPO IN BETHESDA, MD SEPT 14th/15th. IT'S SURE TO BE A REAL SLOBBER-KNOCKER.
(WHERE'S THE BAR?)
COMICS
I AM IRON MAN
DORK IS PUBLISHED ONCE IN A BLUE MOON by SLAVE LABOR GRAPHICS
— 848 the ALAMEDA — SAN JOSE, CA 95126
DAN VADO - PRESIDENTE
BOB SIMPKINS - PUBLISHENTE
VISIT WWW.SLAVELABOR.COM for all your comic book needs
THIS IS
RAN LO
SO THE
NO AD
THE BA
YOU C
CHECK
OUT ON-L
TO SEE NE
HOUSE OF FUN STU
INCLUDING THE FIR
DORK TRADE COLLECT
THE THIRD HECTIC PLAN
TRADE, THE HP BUMM
TRILOGY AND THE MILK
CHEESE BOWLING SHIR
$
HELLO! I'LL BE YOUR TOKEN MONKEY THIS ISSUE!
I HAD THIS DREAM LAST NIGHT... HARVEY KURTZMAN AND A GANG OF SUPERHEROES WERE PULLING ON MY ARMS IN A TUG OF WAR, UNTIL EVENTUALLY THEY TORE ME IN HALF. THEN DOGS ATE MY ENTRAILS. WHAT DOES IT ALL MEAN?
HUH? DID YOU SAY SOME-THING?
MONSTER TIP #
IF YOU GET KILLED BY A MUMMY
YOUR OWN FUCKING FAULT. I ME
C'MON, MUMMIES ARE FUCKIN' SLO
UHHHHHH
WE'RE NOT TALKIN' WOLF
MEN HERE! SO, IF YOU SEE
A MUMMY, JUST-RUN-AWAY!
GIVE IT UP FOR MR. CHIMPY!
CRIPES! EVEN IF MY SHIP DOES COME IN-- LOOK HOW SMALL THAT BASTARD'S GONNA BE!
PSSST! WE'RE GETTING THIRSTY!
CONSIDER YOURSELF WARNED!
CONTENTS ©/TM EVAN DORKIN ANY SIMILARITY TO PERSONS LIVING OR SNUFFED IS A COIN-CIDENCE, OR IS, HEH, SATIRICAL IN NATURE
ELTINGVILLE UBER ALLES!?!
THE ELTINGVILLE CLUB PILOT WE'RE DOING FOR THE CARTOON NETWORK COULD BE DONE BY THE YEAR'S END. WILL IT EVER AIR? WHO THE HELL KNOWS? STAY TUNED!!
HUH?
DORK9 SINGLES JUK
BROADCAST - LET'S GO
NEW PORNOGRAPHERS - LE
FROM AN OCCUPE
ST. ETIENNE - LOSE THAT
NAKED RAYGUN - TREAS
ECHOBELLY - FOUR LETTER W
ALICE DONUT - LISA'S FAT
HOOVERPHONIC - RENAISSANCE AF
OPAL - HAPPY NIGHTMARE BA
THE MUMMIES - PLANET OF THE A
ECHO & THE BUNNYMEN - KILLING M
MAN OR ASTROMAN - RUDY'S LOUNG
STEREO TOTAL - DER SCHLOSSE
and the STATION of the NATION
WFMU - WWW.WFMU.ORG!
SIG
FIRST PRINTING AUGUST 2001
CONTENTS CANNOT BE REPRODUCED W/O PERMISSION, SAVE FOR REVIEWS
PRINTED IN CANADA BY SASQUATCH
CWP

FANBOY CONFESSIONAL
BLESS ME FATHER... I'VE NEVER TOLD THIS TO ANYONE BEFORE--
IT'S ALL RIGHT SON. SPEAK UP.
WELL, I--
--I THINK "THE PHANTOM MENACE" SUCKED!
OH GOD HELP ME!
DR. SUES' "HOW the GRINCH STOLE HANUKKAH!"
OY, SUCH A DEAL I MADE! WHAT SCHMUCKS THOSE WHO-BERGS ARE!
COMIC SHOP CUT-UPS
HEY, KID! THIS AIN'T NO LIBRARY HERE!
OH, REALLY? BUT THE DIRT, THE MESS-- THE STINK OF SWEAT, LONELINESS AND UTTER FAILURE!
I CAN ASSURE YOU SIR, IT WAS AN HONEST MISTAKE!
HOW TO GET SUED: PART 8
TAILS IT IS!
TONIGHT HARVEY DENT FUCKS MEN!
LIVE SEX
NUDE
SEX
REVUE
YOU'VE GOT SHE-MALE XXX
DYSTOPIAN FUNNIES!
IS THIS THE DEPARTMENT OF MISINFORMATION?
NO!
DEPT. OF MIS-INFORMATION
DELIVERIES IN REAR
NO DELIVERIES
BACK IN 5 MIN
CLOSED
JOE 327
NOW PLAYING
PG 1 - MUST I TELL YOU?
PG 2 - "THE SODA THIEF" (FROM THE STREETWISE ANTHOLOGY, 2000)
PG 5 - THE MURDER FAMILY IN -- "APRIL FUNERAL'S DAY"
PG 11 - THE ISLAND OF MISFIT CANDY
PG 13 - THE ELTINGVILLE CLUB IN -- "THE INTERVENTION"
INSIDE BACK COVER -- FUN!
IT'S LIKE I TOLD YOU OFFICER-- I WASN'T SPEEDING-- I WAS HAULING ASS!
ASS
ASS
"HIGHWAY RIBALDRY?!"
DR. SIDNEY GLICK: WORLD'S WORST DERMATOLOGIST!
UFF: I'LL BE RIGHT WITH YOU! UGK
BURGER KING
TWIX
WHY DOES THE NEW YORKER KEEP REJECTING MY CARTOONS?
99¢ SHOP EVERYTHING 99¢ OR LESS!!
99¢
"SO, HOW MUCH FOR A BLOWJOB?"
AMNESTY INTERNATIONAL HOUSE OF PANCAKES
--AND IN THE BACK OF OUR MENU YOU'LL FIND THIS WEEK'S ILLUSTRATED TREATISE ON RAPE AND TORTURE IN THE BALKANS, AND FORCED FEMALE CIRCUMCISION IN AFRICA. SO, CAN I TAKE YOUR ORDER NOW?
WE DO NOT BEAT OUR EGGS
WE DO NOT WHIP OUR BUTTER
AIHOP
DO YOU HAVE "ONLY LOVE CAN BREAK A HEART"?
NOPE.
"THE MAN WHO SHOT LIBERTY VALANCE"?
NUH UH.
"I'M GONNA BE STRONG" "IT HURTS TO BE IN LOVE"? "MECCA"?
NO.
RECORD AND CD WORLD
JOE MEEK
CD CLUB
ROLLING STONE MUSIC FOR 12 YR OLDS
"TOWN WITHOUT PITNEY"

GREETINGS, EVERYONE. WELCOME TO DORK #10. SHARP-EYED READERS WILL NOTICE THAT THIS IS MY FIRST SOLO SERIES TO ACTUALLY HIT A TENTH ISSUE. SHARP-TONGUED READERS WILL NOTICE IT TOOK ME NEARLY 10 YRS TO GET HERE.
ANYWAY, I'D LIKE TO TAKE THIS WORD BALLOON TO THANK ALL OF YOU WHO WROTE IN REGARDING THE "WELCOME TO ELTINGVILLE" "SPECIAL" (i.e, FAILED PILOT), THAT AIRED RECENTLY ON THE CARTOON NETWORK.
SARAH AND I CERTAINLY APPRECIATED THE SUPPORT FOR THE SHOW/SHOW OF SUPPORT. AS FOR THE FUTURE OF THE ELTINGVILLE CLUB, I'M WORKING ON A ONE-SHOT COMIC FOR NEXT YEAR, WHICH WILL MOST LIKELY BE THEIR FINAL MEETING. I THINK.
AFTER THAT, WHO KNOWS? I HAVE A HABIT OF NOT FOLLOWING UP ON THINGS, SO I'M JUST HAPPY I GOT THIS SUCKER DONE. HOPE YOU LIKE IT-- IF NOT, WELL, YOU KNOW WHERE YOU CAN GO. HA! ONLY KIDDING! I THINK.
BOOSKA IS LORD
VISIT THE HOUSE OF FUN!
WWW.HOUSEOFFUN.COM
FOR MORE INFO ON WHAT WE
WHY ARE YOU READING ALL THIS CRAP?
WFMU
SHIT YOU SHOULD HAVE FINISHED BY NOW, PUTZ!
THE THING-NIGHT FALLS ON YANCY ST.-SCRIPTS #3/4
THAT BIZARRO SCRIPT for JOEY
FLAME RITE ZIPPO ART BOOK-???
ACTION GIRL CO-ED BOOK-LETTERING/etc
ELTINGVILLE ONE-SHOT-2 STRIPS?!?
THAT SCRIPT I PITCHED to AXEL-??
M&C #8? HA HA! RIGHT!
2ND DORK TRADE-APRIL? MAY?
SLG
CWP
AUG 18th!
LETTER ONE-PUNCH FOR THE CO-ED SPECIAL!
MR CHIMPY GETS LEGAL!
CONTENTS © EVAN DORKIN, 2002. ANY SIMILARITY TO PERSONS, PUPPETS OR CHIMPS-- LIVING OR DEAD--IS COINCIDENTAL OR A SATIRICAL TYPE DEAL
DON'T CLUTTER THE PAGE!
COLORING, SEPS, PRE-PRESS, COMPUTER STUFF, SMARTS AND SAVVY: SARAH DYER
OUR BOY IS INDEED LUCKY SHE HAS NOT KILLED HIM BY NOW.
DORK IS PUBLISHED ONCE A YEAR AT BEST by SLAVE LABOR GRAPHICS
DAN VADO prez
BOB SIMPKINS pub
DORK #10 by evan dorkin po box 060380 staten island new york 10306
EVANDORKIN@AOL.COM
MOMMY SEZ I DRAW PURTY!
PRINTED IN CANADA FIRST PRINTING - SEPT 2002
DON'T LIKE MY COMICS? DIAL 1-800-EAT-SHIT
SLG CONTACT INFO
WWW.SLAVELABOR.COM
PO BOX 26427 SAN JOSE, CA 95159-
CALL DAN 4 $

I'M SORRY, MR. HALL, BUT THE TESTS CAME BACK POSITIVE. YOU'RE A FUCKING MORON.
OH GOD! I KNEW IT!
I'VE ONLY BEEN INTO JESUS FOR A FEW YEARS NOW, BUT I'M LIKE, REALLY INTO HIM, Y'KNOW?
PASSOVER WITH THE SELF-LOATHING JEWS
PASS THE MATZOH, YOU CHEAP BASTARD!
PASS A KIDNEY STONE, YOU KIKE SON OF A BITCH, YOU!
HEY, LADY DO YOU MIND? WE'RE TRYING TO EAT HERE! LOUSY SHIKSA.
THE WHAT AND THE WHERE!
PG 1 - YOU'RE READING IT
PG 2 - MORE ADVERTISING CHARACTERS OF YESTERYEAR
PG 4 - THE ELTINGVILLE CLUB IN - "AS SEEN ON T.V."
PG 9 - MIGHTY CARL JUNG
PG 12 - HOW TO GET YOUR ASS KICKED IN 5 E-Z LESSONS
PG 17 - THE DEVIL PUPPET'S INVISIBLE COLLEGE
SEND UP the CLOWNS
WELL, TIM'S NOT FUNNY, AND BOB'S NOT FUNNY, AND I SURE AS HELL AIN'T FUNNY...
SHIT! ARE ANY OF US FUNNY?
F See me!!
Book Report on 2 Years B 4 the Mast by Prince, 5th grade
2 Years B 4 the Mast is about a student who wa 2 B a sailor. U see, he had measles 2 the point w almost died, so
MAYBE I WANTED SOMETHIN' T'DRINK YA FUCKIN' FUCKBAG BITCHDICK SHIT SHIT SHITTER SHIT COCKSUCKER BASTARD!
TOMMY O'TOOLE (AND TRENCHMOUTH) TOURETTE'S VENTRILOQUIST
"ORGY LAFFS"
YOU'LL EXCUSE ME WHILE I SLIP INTO SOMEONE MORE COMFORTABLE.
K-Y
DR. SIDNEY GLICK: WORLD'S WORST SEX THERAPIST
WELL, TO BE HONEST, I WOULDN'T FUCK HER EITHER.
DR GLICK
OH MY!
HEY, BABY! WANNA DATE?
WE IS HERE WE IS HERE WE IS HERE!
HEY, BIG BOY, LOOKIN' FOR COMPANY?
HORTON HEARS a HO!
COMMIE "GAG" I WROTE IN '55
"GET HIM -- THE LIFE OF THE PARTY."

OBLIGATORY DORK #6 AUDIO PLAYLIST 2000

THE REPLACEMENTS - ALL FOR NOTHING
MY BLOODY VALENTINE - LOVELESS
ROCKET FROM the CRYPT - THE STATE OF ART IS ON FIRE
SERVOTRON - NO ROOM FOR HUMANS
THEE HEADCOATS - HEAVENS to MURGATROID...
THE KINKS - SOMETHING ELSE BY THE KINKS
BIMSKALABIM - BIMSKALABIM
STEREOLAB - EMPEROR TOMATO KETCHUP
THE PSYCHADELIC FURS - ALL OF THIS AND NOTHING
HENRY MANCINI - DAYS OF WINE AND ROSES

I DIG THAT SOUND!

WFMU 91.1 FM NJ http://www.wfmu.org

UPCOMING

2 TRADE PAPERBACKS OF ALL MY OUT-OF-PRINT PIRATE CORP$! HECTIC PLANET COMICS FROM '87-'92. (AUG)

WHO CARES

NEW EPISODES OF SPACE GHOST COAST TO COAST BY SARAH AND I. (AUG)

COLORSTRIPS WE DID FOR DHC'S SCATTERBRAIN SERIES.

GEORGINA AND DEVIL PUPPET ZIPPOS FROM SMOKE KING.

MY POORLY ATTENDED FUNERAL

"MAKE WAY FOR DULL MINUTIAE"

©98 JOE HACK

FOR SEMI-UPDATED INFO ON OUR TV AND COMICS PROJECTS, CHECK OUT THE HOUSE OF FUN WEB SITE! HTTP://WWW.houseoffun.com

DORK IS PUBLISHED BY SLAVE LABOR GRAPHICS

DAN VADO - KING KONG
CRAIG PAPE - MIGHTY JOE YOUNG
MAX GAULT - GENERAL URKO
CHRISTINA BORELLO - DR ZIRA

FOR A FREE SLAVE LABOR GRAPHICS CATALOGUE CALL 1-800 866-8929 OR WRITE - 325 S. FIRST ST. #301 SAN JOSE CA, 95113

FIRST PRINTING - MAY '98

PRINTED IN CANADA

THANKS FOR YOUR SUPPORT

WE'RE LOOKING FOR SOMEONE TO PLAY WITH...

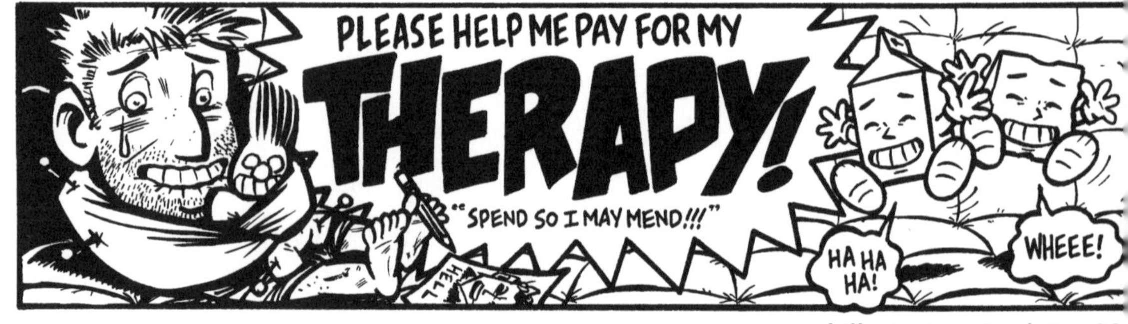

ad illustration, *Dork* 7, 199

HAPPY BIRTHDAY TO ME

website-only Fun strip, April 200

LOOK! LOOK el VIBORA READERS!

LOOK WHAT I DID!

NOW HE'S REALLY WORTHLESS IN THAT CONDITION!

GOD DAMMIT! WE WANTED TO DO THAT!

AT LEAST LET US HAVE THE HEAD FOR OUR WORLD CUP GAME!

H-HI K-KIDS...

EV/02

promotional sketch for Spanish magazine *El Vibora*, 2002

Cluttered Like My Sketchbook: *Dork* character designs, layout roughs, and doodles.

JUNG!
FOLKS! PLEASE
YES! CAPN
THIS
BUS STOP
WE SHOULD HAVE CALLED A CAB.
I TOLD YOU, WE DON'T HAVE ENOUGH MONEY FOR A CAB.
I'M COLD.

YOU, I, the entire cosmos. All of us are
CIRCLING the DRAIN
TITLE PAGE? by evan dorkin
DRAW MORE LIKE THIS

HA
HA
HA
YOU'LL LAUGH
YOU'LL CRY
AND THEN YOU'LL WONDER...
WHY
?
DORK
INK
BE FUNNY
HMPH.
HUH.
HA! HAR!
HMM.
HUH?
HA!
DORK
DORK
BE
FUNNY
NOW!
BEER
DRAWING A BLANK

COMIC BOOK STORE
IF YOU DON'T SEE IT- WE DON'T IT!
NO KIDS IN SHOP
NO GIRLS ALOWED
HOURS BY WHIM
HEY, MR. CHIMPY! SAY--WHY THE LONG FACE?

I'M A CHIMP. CHIMPS HAVE LONG FACES. BUT YOU'RE RIGHT, I AM BUMMED OUT. MY CRAPPY LOCAL COMICS SHOP WON'T CARRY MY FAVORITE HUMOR TITLES! I ASKED THE OWNER TO ORDER THEM, BUT HE JUST GRUNTED AND WENT BACK TO HIS MAGIC GAME!

AT CAN I DO TO GET E COMICS I WANT?
DON'T FRET, CHUM! YOU CAN GET ALL THE EVAN DORKIN COMICS YOU WANT STRAIGHT FROM THE PUBLISHER!
GUESS I WON'T TELL MR. BUNNY MY FAVORITE HUMOR ARTIST IS IVAN BRUNETTI!

AND THERE'S PLENTY OF NEAT STUFF TO CHOOSE FROM, TOO! FIRST OFF, THERE'S DORK! THE AWARD-WINNING HUMOR ANTHOLOGY FEATURING THE DEVIL PUPPET, the MURDER FAMILY, FUN STRIPS, FISHER-PRICE THEATRE AND MORE! I LIKE #7 FEATURING EVAN'S REAL-LIFE NERVOUS BREAKDOWN! TOO FUNNY! THERE'S TEN ISSUES, A TRADE COLLECTION, EVEN T-SHIRTS!
DORK

REMEMBER THE "WELCOME TO ELTINGVILLE" ANIMATED PILOT ON THE CARTOON NETWORK?
uh, NO, ACTUALLY. DID THAT AIR--?
WELL, THAT WAS BASED ON THE ELTINGVILLE CLUB STRIPS FROM DORK #6! THE CLUB'S ALSO IN ISSUES #3, 4, 8 and 9! AND, YES, THERE'S A T-SHIRT OF THEM, ALSO!!
DORK

AND LET'S NOT FORGET MILK and CHEESE! THOSE BELOVED LITTLE MONSTERS WHO LOVE TO HATE, LIVE TO HATE, AND HATE TO LOSE! THERE'S 7 ISSUES, A TRADE, AND BESIDES THE OBLIGATORY T-SHIRTS, AN EXCLUSIVE M&C BOWLING SHIRT!
MILK CHEESE
BLAH BLAH!

MIGHT ALSO WANT TO CHECK HECTIC PLANET, the SLICE OF URE LIFE SLAPSTICK ROMANCE IC WITH A SKA/PUNK BACKBEAT. EE TRADES ARE AVAILABLE, PLUS ONE SHOT "BUMMER TRILOGY."
THERE'S ALSO ANOMALIES LIKE the ALL-AGES KID BLASTOFF AND the ADULTS-ONLY DICK WAD OF THE MEGA VICE SQUAD!

ICK!
DICK WAD
HEY, WHO ARE THOSE GUYS? THEY DON'T LOOK LIKE COMIC BOOK FANS!
OH, THOSE ARE F.B.I. AGENTS. I TOLD THEM MR. RETAILER DEALS IN CHILD PORNOGRAPHY.
DOES HE?

DOES IT MATTER? THE COMMUNITY ALREADY HAS ITS SUSPICIONS-- ALL THEY KNOW IS GROWN MEN WALK IN AND OUT OF HIS SHOP WITH MAGAZINES AND VIDEO TAPES IN PLAIN PAPER BAGS.

CHARGE WON'T STICK, BUT HE'LL GO ER FIGHTING IT. Hmmm... I WONDER E'LL CALL the COMIC BOOK LEGAL ENSE FUND, EVEN THOUGH HE DOESN'T PORT IT? I'LL NIP THAT IN THE BUD!
UNSOLD COMICS MAKE FOR GREAT KINDLING...
CLOSED
THIS SEEMS WRONG.

REMEMBER, KIDS, SOME COMIC SHOPS ARE SWELL as HELL!* BUT MOST ARE SWIRLING BLACK PITS of DEBT, FILTH and INCOMPETENCE! IF YOUR LOCAL SHOP SUCKS EGGS and YOU CAN'T GET COMICS LIKE DORK EASILY, THEN JUST TAKE YOUR MONEY DIRECTLY to SLAVE LABOR GRAPHICS! It's e-z! SHOP ONLINE @ WWW.SLAVELABOR.COM! OR ORDER BY PHONE w/a CREDIT CARD at 1-800-866-8929 CATALOGUES are AVAILABLE UPON REQUEST ONLINE, by PHONE, OR BY WRITING SLG at: PO BOX 26427, SAN JOSE CA 95159-6427
ORDER NOW!
ORDER OFTEN!

AND TELL THEM YOUR CRAPPY LOCAL COMIC SHOP SENT YOU!

DORK #10

* LIKE THE ONE YOU BOUGHT THIS COMIC AT!